This Book

COVERING THE
BASICS

is presented to

_____

By _____

Message _____

_____

_____

Date _____

COVERING THE
BASICS

A GUIDE FOR
UPCOMING LEADERS
IN MINISTRY

JOAN HUNTER &
MELODY BARKER

Covering the Basics: A Guide for Upcoming Leaders in Ministry
ISBN: 978-0-9829516-3-7

Copyright © 2012 by Joan Hunter and Melody Barker

Published by Hunter Books
PO Box 411
Pinehurst, TX 77362 USA
www.joanhunter.org

Cover design by Yvonne Parks at www.pearcreative.ca
Interior design by David Sluka at www.hitthemarkpublishing.com

Printed in the United States of America

Contents

Introduction 7

1. Salvation 9

2. Baptism of the Holy Spirit 15

3. Water Baptism 19

4. Communion 33

5. Foot Washing 57

6. Ministry Event Guidelines 63

7. Receiving Offerings for Your Ministry 67

8. Marriage Ceremony 75

9. Renewing Marital Vows 93

10. House Dedication 95

11. Baby Dedication 101

12. Graduation 105

13. Building Dedication 107

14. Funeral 111

Notes 123

Introduction

WE ARE EXCITED about presenting this book to you as a believer who has been called into a greater level of ministry. Many times newly ordained or commissioned believers are asked to do a wedding and their excited response is "Yes! Sure!" Then they have no clue how to proceed. Not to mention a funeral or any of the other ceremonies that we have in this book.

It can be overwhelming to look on the Internet and try to find the right reference or the traditional phrase for a wedding, not to mention knowing what to say at a funeral, or how to pray and dedicate a building, house, or baby. In this creative and collaborative work, we have given you at outline to enable you to move forward in ministry.

It is designed as an outline, reference, or tool to help you follow through on the God's call on your life. These can be followed verbatim or changed up for specific situations. Feel free to add some of your personality to it. After you have done them many times, you won't need to refer to them.

The vision of Joan Hunter Ministries is to train and equip believers to take the healing power of God beyond the 4 walls of the church and go into the 4 corners of the earth. Through this collection of ceremonies, you will have greater preparation for going into the 4 corners of the earth.

I want to encourage you to read through this book and pray and ask God for your own additions. Ask God for verses to come to you and allow Him to reveal to you more revelation than what is even in these pages.

God bless you as you continue in the call on your life.

Salvation
The Greatest Gift of All

"For God so loved the world, that He gave His only begotten Son, that whoever believes in Him shall not perish, but have eternal life." John 3:16

WELCOMING JESUS CHRIST as Lord and Savior is the greatest miracle anyone can experience. Accepting God's Son into an open and willing heart is truly receiving the greatest gift of all. Therefore, what a privilege it is to lead someone to a saving knowledge of Jesus Christ.

Explain God's Love for All to Understand

The most important element of evangelism is the love of God for sinful man. Explaining that love to the lost in a language they understand is always the challenge. Despite our sin, God loves us. He will never leave us or forsake us. No matter how bad we have been, He still loves us because we are His children, His creation. As Christians, we love Him because He first loved us and sacrificed His only Son for our sins thousands of years before we were born. Because Jesus now lives within us, we can choose to love others because we know how much He loves them as well.

John 3:16 will always be an important verse in sharing the gospel with non-Christians. All the essential elements of the gospel are contained in this one verse: God's loving provision for sinful man and man's need to understand it by faith and enter into His eternal blessings. The rest of the Bible explains what John wrote in one short verse.

Everyone Needs Salvation

"For all have sinned, and come short of the glory of God." Romans 3:23

We have all sinned. We have all done things that are displeasing to God. No one is innocent. The punishment that we have earned for our sins is death. We earned these wages by our own decisions, our own ignorance and blinded eyes. Eternal life is a free gift. Jesus has made a way. He has opened the door to the throne room for us.

"For the wages of sin is death; but the gift of God is eternal life through Jesus Christ our Lord." Romans 6:23

"But God demonstrates His own love toward us, in that while we were still sinners, Christ died for us." Romans 5:8

Jesus Christ died to pay the price of our sins. God provided a way to be reconciled to Him before we were even born.

"...for everyone who calls on the name of the Lord
will be saved." Romans 10:13

Jesus died to pay for our sins and rescue us from damnation and hell. Salvation and forgiveness of sin is freely given to all who believe. Anyone who trusts in Jesus Christ and calls on His name, as Lord and Savior, they will be saved. No age limit. No qualifying criteria. Anyone at anytime, anywhere can call on His name. Even with a final breath before death, God hears a final request.

"...that if you confess with your mouth
Jesus as Lord, and believe in your heart that God
raised Him from the dead, you will be saved."
Romans 10:9

Because of Jesus' death on the cross, simply believing in Him, and trusting His death as the payment for our sins opens our hearts to Him. The blackness of our hearts is replaced with the purity of Jesus' heart and His salvation. God honors our testimony of faith in Christ's work and saves us from the penalties of sin. It is important to make a public confession of our decision.

The Benefits of Salvation

"Therefore, since we have been justified through
faith, we have peace with God through our Lord
Jesus Christ." Romans 5:1

Through Jesus Christ, we can find peace. God is peace. Follow peace. Follow God.

"Therefore, there is now no condemnation for those who are in Christ Jesus." Romans 8:1

Because Jesus died on the cross to pay for the sins of all mankind, believers will never be condemned for their sins. Eternity will be spent with Him in heaven. Now His Holy Spirit lives within us.

"For I am convinced that neither death nor life, neither angels nor demons, neither the present nor the future, nor any powers, neither height nor depth, nor anything else in all creation, will be able to separate us from the love of God that is in Christ Jesus our Lord." Romans 8:38-39

By faith in Jesus Christ, a person receives God's free gift of love and life. Believing is simply trusting God's Word. With our heart, we believe that Jesus is God's Son who died for our sin on the cross and arose from the grave to live in us as Savior and Lord.

Questions before Salvation Prayer

- If you believe in Jesus, will you confess your faith with the words you speak?
- Do you admit that you are a sinner?
- Do you believe that Jesus, God's Son, died for your sins on the cross?
- Will you turn away from your old life and accept new eternal life with Him?

Prayer of Salvation

If you want to receive Jesus Christ into your heart as your Lord and Savior, repeat after me. (Remember to allow time for them to repeat the part you said. Find the natural break in the prayer. Lead them slowly so that they will think about the words they are saying, without worrying about forgetting the words you just said).

Prayer Option

Father, I know that I have sinned. I ask you now to separate my sins from me and put them on the cross. I am truly sorry for what I have done in the past. Today, I turn away from my sins and embrace all You have for me. I believe that Your Son, Jesus Christ, died on the cross for my sins, was resurrected from the dead, and is alive forevermore.

Prayer Option

Jesus, I ask You to forgive me of my sins. I invite You to become the Lord of my life. Today I choose to give you my whole heart. I ask You now to rule and reign in my heart and life from this day forward. Father, through Your Holy Spirit, lead me and guide me into *all* You have for me. In Jesus' name I pray, amen.

Baptism of the Holy Spirit

Your Heavenly Language

Now that Jesus Christ is your Lord and Savior, ask for the baptism of the Holy Spirit. He will empower you to do His will. Scripture tells us that when He fills you, He also gives you the gift of speaking in "unknown tongues."

"Speaking in tongues" simply means the Holy Spirit speaks through a willing vessel: a human who trusts Him enough to speak a language they have neither learned or understand. To the nonbeliever, the words may sound like gibberish or nonsense. To the believer, the words become the language of heaven.

Paul said, *"I will pray with the spirit and I will pray with the understanding. I will sing with the spirit, and I will also sing with the understanding"* (1 Corinthians 14:15).

Paul also said, *"I thank my God I speak with tongues more than you all"* (1 Corinthians 14:18).

> *"But you will receive power when the Holy Spirit comes on you; and you will be my witnesses in*

*Jerusalem, and in all Judea and Samaria, and to the
ends of the earth." Acts 1:8*

When you pray in tongues, you pray in the perfect will of God. When you don't know what to pray or how to pray over a situation, pray in tongues. God gives you the words to speak.

Prayer to Receive the Baptism of the Holy Spirit

Lord Jesus, I thank You for the most exciting gift of all—the gift of salvation. Jesus, You promised another gift, the gift of the Holy Spirit. So I ask You, Father, to baptize me with the Holy Spirit right now, exactly as you did your disciples on the day of Pentecost. Thank You, Jesus! You have done Your part and now I am going to do my part. I am going to lift my hands up to You, God (lift your hands); I am going to look up to You. I will praise You, but not in any language I know because I can't speak two languages at one time. Father, I love You; I praise You; I worship You; I love You with all of my heart.

Now lift up your hands. Praise Him. Allow His Spirit speak through you. Don't use the words you know. Make the small, perhaps odd sounds you feel bubble up through your spirit. Let those "sounds" flow out of your mouth. Don't try to interpret anything, just allow your mouth to express itself. Start speaking those sounds faster and faster.

Stop! You can stop and start these sounds or words anytime you choose. Start again. After a few minutes, stop again! This wonderful gift can be expressed loudly or softly. You can even think in tongues or pray silently using His Spiritual language. Singing in tongues is also a wonderful experience. When many believers gather together, singing in tongues truly becomes like a heavenly chorus with perfect music and harmony. Try it. (Sing in tongues.)

Look forward to a wonderful experience with the Holy Spirit. Your understanding will increase. Your prayer language will be powerful. Your discernment and understanding will soar as you allow Him to flow through you.

God's Word talks about the tongue, how unruly and hard it is to tame. It is the last holdout of control. Once you allow God's Holy Spirit to take control of your tongue (your words), miracles follow.

Water Baptism

3

SCRIPTURALLY, BAPTISM was first explained in the Gospels of the New Testament. John, Jesus' cousin, was best known as John the Baptist. He traveled through the Judean countryside as a forerunner to the Messiah, calling people to repent and return to God and a godly lifestyle. As a sign of their repentance, they were baptized with water in the Jordan River.

Even though John was clothed with camel's hair held together by a leather belt and ate locusts for food, the people came, listened, were baptized, and followed him. Later research indicates he probably lived in the desert, coming to civilization at the appointed time to prepare the way for Christ to start His ministry.

> *"John came baptizing in the wilderness and preaching a baptism of repentance for the remission of sins. Then all the land of Judea, and those from Jerusalem, went out to him and were all baptized by him in the Jordan River, confessing their sins."*
> *Mark 1:4-5*

"I indeed baptize you with water unto repentance,
but He who is coming after me is mightier than
I, whose sandals I am not worthy to carry. He
will baptize you with the Holy Spirit and fire."
Matthew 3:5-6, 11

John Baptized Jesus

Jesus went to the Jordan River to meet with John because John had a role to play in His destiny. John's first reaction was to say, "No, I can't do this." John knew who Jesus was and did not feel worthy to baptize Him. Jesus encouraged John by telling him that this was necessary to fulfill all righteousness.

What a privilege, what an honor, what amazement John must have felt when he realized who Jesus was. They had spent time growing up together and John probably recognized that Jesus was different from the other rowdy, normal boys. Suddenly, he is asked to baptize this special man. How does one ask the Son of God to repent of His sins when He had been perfect His entire life? John probably felt speechless, but he did know how to obey the voice of God.

Then Jesus came from Galilee to John at the Jordan to be baptized by him. And John tried to prevent Him, saying, "I need to be baptized by You, and are You coming to me?"

"But Jesus answered and said to him, 'Permit it to
be so now, for thus it is fitting for us to fulfill all
righteousness.' Then he allowed Him. When He had
been baptized, Jesus came up immediately from the
water; and behold, the heavens were opened to Him,

*and He saw the Spirit of God descending like a dove
and alighting upon Him."* Matthew 3:13-16

Jesus' baptism was an important event in His life. The heavens opened and the Holy Spirit of God descended from the Father's throne and landed on Him. God spoke from heaven and announced to the world that Jesus was indeed His beloved Son.

*"And suddenly a voice came from heaven, saying,
'This is My beloved Son, in whom I am well
pleased.'"* Matthew 3:17

Many believe this is when the Holy Spirit empowered Jesus to enter into His ministry and to fulfill the ancient Scriptures.

Today, even though the word "baptism" means immersion and can be used to describe other experiences, the actual term is usually connected to a religious rite of the church. During this important sacrament, a person is immersed under the water. Some denominations sprinkle a few drops of anointed water on the person's head or forehead. Many committed, born-again Christians welcome and want total immersion baptism some time during their life.

Salvation without Baptism

If a person is not baptized, is he or she going to hell? Nothing in the Bible indicates anyone is totally lost without this experience. I don't believe God will ban any true believer from passing through His pearly gates if they have not been dipped, dunked, or sprinkled with water. Before the age of accountability, infants and children certainly are not doomed if they are not baptized before they die. Those who believe salvation is only possible through baptism have baptized babies for centuries. Although in recent years baby dedications have replaced infant baptism in many churches.

"He who believes and is baptized will be saved; but he who does not believe will be condemned."
Mark 16:16

Baptism is a vital part of a Christian's life even though few actually understand its underlying spiritual meaning. To many, being baptized is recognized as an outward expression of repentance of sin and salvation. This is certainly true, but the underlying spiritual meaning of baptism goes much farther than the world can see.

Following repentance and asking Jesus to come into one's heart, commonly known as salvation, a new believer is encouraged to be baptized. Many follow this advice without understanding the spiritual meaning. It may be years before an adequate explanation or revelation opens spiritual eyes to what actually happened when they were immersed in water to emerge a new person in Christ.

Why Do We Get Baptized?

One may say we are to follow the Lord's example. Repent, ask Him into our hearts, and be baptized. Yes, that is one good reason. As explained earlier, baptism is an outward sign to the world that one has accepted Jesus as Savior and has become a Christian.

In reality, the act of being baptized goes much further than just something a new believer does as a sign to the world. When a person goes underwater, what happens? Swimmers know very well that a person cannot breathe underwater. Without air, the body dies.

Baptism is that point and place where you put aside the old self. You turn away from the world and focus your entire life on God. Going completely under the water is a symbolic death. During baptism, you are willingly giving up your old sinful life. You are letting the water wash away all the junk you have been carrying around your whole life. Yes, the sin is washed away and you will emerge as white as snow.

Red Blood Shed on the Cross

+

Blackness of your Sin

=

Pure White Snow

Amazing formula, isn't it?

Christianity today tends to focus on all the benefits of salvation, but you cannot have those benefits until you first choose to die to self. You must first go down, in order to come back up. Resurrection life requires a death, your death. First you die, and then you receive His resurrection life.

Not only do you lose your old life, you will also lose all the lies of the enemy. When he comes to whisper in your ear and remind you of the things you did in the past, you can say, "No, that wasn't me. I am a new person! That was the old me! I am clean! I belong to God, not YOU! You are no longer my master!"

Baptism symbolizes your choice, not only to others, but also to God. When you go under the water, you are making a definitive statement to the principalities and powers of this world, just as Jesus did. You are telling the rulers of darkness and this fallen world that you are dying to the things they offer. You are choosing a new way of living. There is no middle ground—living with one foot in the world and one foot in heaven. You are saying, "No" to the kingdom of darkness and "Yes" to the kingdom of Light!

> *"For as the body is one and has many members, but all the members of that one body, being many, are one body, so also is Christ. For by one Spirit we were all baptized into one body—whether Jews or Greeks, whether slaves or free—and have all been made to drink into one Spirit."*
> *1 Corinthians 12:12-13*

> *"Therefore we were buried with Him through baptism into death, that just as Christ was raised from the dead by the glory of the Father, even so we also should walk in newness of life." Romans 6:4*

God wants the old you to go under the water and emerge looking like His Son, Jesus. Emerging out of the water, you have another chance at life, a new life, a new beginning. Do you realize that when you ask Jesus into your heart, you become a new creation? You have Jesus and His Spirit living within you. The person you once were has died. You have given your body, your mind and your spirit to Him. God recreates you into the Body of Christ. You choose to give your "self" away and accept Jesus into your being.

"Jesus answered, 'Most assuredly, I say to you, unless one is born of water and the Spirit, he cannot enter the kingdom of God.'" John 3:5

Accepting Jesus as Savior, being baptized, and allowing Jesus to have full control of your life is all part of being a born again Christian. You have to make the choice.

"Jesus answered and said to him, 'Most assuredly, I say to you, unless one is born again, he cannot see the kingdom of God.'" John 3:3

"Do not marvel that I said to you, 'You must be born again.'" John 3:7

"Having been born again, not of corruptible seed but incorruptible, through the word of God, which lives and abides forever." 1 Peter 1:23

Who Baptizes?

John the Baptist started the age-old tradition of baptism. He did not belong to any church or group of believers. Today, baptism does not belong exclusively to any one person or group of people either. Even though the head of a church or religious organization usually baptizes people, this practice is still man-made. Yes, it is considered a Sacrament of the Church; however, baptizing someone is not limited to the Christian leaders and pastors.

Once John was thrown into prison and subsequently be-headed, did baptism stop? No. The message of repentance was preached by John's followers, as well as Jesus, who started His ministry at that time. The next question is: "Did Jesus do all the baptizing?" No, He didn't.

> *"Therefore, when the Lord knew that the Pharisees had heard that Jesus made and baptized more disciples than John. (Even though Jesus Himself did not baptize, but His disciples.)" John 4:1-2*

Jesus taught and instructed His disciples how to minister in all necessary ways before His death. He equipped His followers to continue His work. He knew His death was imminent. He didn't leave His followers ill prepared.

Immersion is Not an Option

As a follower of Christ in today's world, you need to be equipped to follow the disciple's example. Study, learn, share, and do. Learn what baptism really means. Share what you learn with others. Then if someone wants to be baptized, be comfortable ministering to them.

In cases where baptism is requested for a child or an adult who cannot be immersed, know that the "sprinkle" method is acceptable. They can always be immersed later if they choose. Occasionally, you may be called to minister to a homebound or hospitalized person. Don't say, "No" to their sincere request. "Sprinkle."

Understand that God is making the change in the person, not you. You don't have to preach a sermon. Allow them to express their profession of Christ as their Savior, that He indeed lives within their heart. Then follow Jesus' instructions: ***Baptize them in the name of the Father, the Son and of the Holy Spirit.***

"Go therefore and make disciples of all the nations, baptizing them in the name of the Father and of the Son and of the Holy Spirit." Matthew 28:19

Through the death of our flesh (baptism), God cancels out sin by our identification with Christ's death. God supernaturally cancels our sin. When we emerge from the water, we identify with His resurrection. By faith, we enter into the power of His resurrection. We celebrate baptism as the covenant sign of our entering into a new life. It is for anyone who has made the commitment to serve Christ with all of their heart.

Preparation for Water Baptism

- Have you died to your old self, that is, who you used to be before salvation?
- Are you prepared to be a brand new person alive with Christ?
- Are you ready to die to yourself and live for Him?
- Welcome to His Body.

Water Baptism Ceremony

Baptism is a voluntary commitment made by believers in obedience to Jesus' command. It is a public act commonly recognized by the body of Christ as a symbol of the new birth; a turning point in a person's life as they joyfully enter God's kingdom of light.

Water baptism is normally done by immersion, which means the person goes under the surface of water and rises out again, symbolizing the new birth in Christ. Water baptism can be done in swimming pools, creeks, lakes, oceans or large tubs. Many churches have baptismal pools behind or under a church platform: but baptism is a public ceremony that can be conducted anywhere as long as there is enough water.

Most baptisms will have someone else in the water with the new Christian. The attendant is usually a minister, but can also be a family member or close friend. Most new believers are immersed once; however, in some areas of the world, the new Christian is immersed three times.

As Jesus directed in the Scripture, we baptize in the name of the Father, Son and Holy Spirit. Some traditions do not refer to all three members of the Godhead; there is no strict rule to follow. We simply choose to follow Jesus' instructions.

The officiating minister may use the occasion to give a brief teaching on the importance and meaning of the ceremony. If time permits, and with the new Christian's permission, the person doing the service may say a few words about the conversion experience of the individual being baptized.

Directions for Water Baptism

- The person ministering assists the new believer by lowering him or her backward into the water.
- The participant holds their nose with one hand and holds the other wrist with the second hand.

- The minister holds the head with one hand while the other hand holds a wrist as the person goes backwards into the water.

- Sometimes, the participant being baptized kneels in the water and is assisted to lie back into the water. Then the minister will help lift them out of the water. (This can be a very emotional experience and the participant may be a little unsteady or nervous.)

- Depending on the size of the baptismal pool, the minister may have to assist the candidate in and out of the pool.

- If possible, have others available to assist the participant during entry and exit of the baptismal area.

Recommended Supplies

- Participants should bring an extra set of clothes to change into before the baptism, as well as have a dry change of clothes for after the baptism. (Some people may want to wear white. Recommend or require underclothing under any white fabric, as they will be wet after the immersion.)

- Caution them not to use any lightweight fabric, which can become very transparent and embarrassing when wet.

- Encourage them to wear flip-flops or other waterproof footwear to protect their feet.

- Bring one or two towels for yourself.

- Bring a bag to put wet immersion clothes and towels into after immersion ceremony is conducted.
- Slip proof material around the baptismal area will prevent any falls or injuries on wet walkways.

During baptism in the Jordan River in Israel, many people are baptized at the same time. Jesus' words are spoken over the entire group before immersion. Those being baptized control their own entry and exit from the water. Whether they immerse themselves once or many times is their choice.

No matter what the details of the ceremony, baptism is a very life changing experience.

Preparation

- Ensure that the participant is saved—a believer in Jesus Christ.
- Make sure that the participant voluntarily chooses to be baptized.
- Check to see that the participant understands what baptism means.
- Make sure that proper clothing and footwear is available.
- Keep towels and extra robes for those who forget to bring their own.
- Use safe walkways with adequate lighting.
- It is best if the pool or baptismal area is large enough for one to two people to be immersed. Water should be at least four feet deep for adults, three feet deep for children.

- Have fresh clean water in the pool or baptismal area, at a comfortable temperature.
- Create a comfortable environmental temperature, not too hot or cold.
- Invite witnesses. The family should be invited. The occasion may be an answer to someone's prayers. Or perhaps the event will be a witness to the unsaved members of the family.
- Prior to service, have the participant ask a family member or friend take pictures or record the immersion ceremony.

Immersion Ceremony

After their public confession of faith, have them hold their nose with one hand. With their other hand they should grasp their wrist. This stabilizes their hands as well as keeps water from going up their nose during immersion. Gently but firmly grasp their wrist with your stronger hand, meanwhile placing your other hand on their back to support them during the plunge.

Their hands have made a good support for you to hold onto while they are immersed. Brace yourself with your legs as you lower them backwards into the water and then bring them back up, using both the strength of your legs and use of both of your arms.

If you have children or have friends that are willing to let you practice on them, it would be a good idea. Immersion is not hard but you want to make sure you can do it in a comfortable way.

Baptize Them in the Name of the Father, the Son and of the Holy Spirit

As you say these words, baptize them:

"Go therefore and make disciples of all the nations, baptizing them in the name of the Father and of the Son and of the Holy Spirit." Matthew 28:19

Communion

4

EVERYONE HAS BEEN INVITED to dinner at some point during his or her life. At home, we are simply called to the dinner table; however, for special occasions, or to gather with friends, an invitation is offered. Meetings are held to discuss important matters or to talk over a coffee or tea. Dinner has a more important meaning.

Dinners can be for thousands or just a few. Large, sit down dinners are usually impersonal, loud, and noisy. Small intimate dinners are so special and more unique. Personal information is exchanged. Joy, merriment, laughter, smiles, and peace abound as friends grow closer together by sharing a moment of food and drink.

A very special dinner was planned over two thousand years ago: the Host called His best friends together in a special room prepared just for the occasion. The Host prepared the evening's menu very carefully. Every item had a significant meaning. Every word spoken by the Host would live forever throughout time.

The Host was happy to be surrounded by His friends, but at the same time, He was sad. He knew His friends would soon be changed. They would be filled with fear, dread, worry, pain, despair, depression, doubt, and grief. One would soon be dead. Yes, He knew what was going to happen to the men who had faithfully followed Him across the countryside for the last three years.

He also knew He had to follow His Father's will. He had His marching orders and had to walk into Hell itself in order to save the world. So, He served the bread and wine. He spoke His final intimate instructions to these select few and His destiny was fulfilled.

The men had no idea this would be their final night together. After all, their Host had told them He was the Son of God! Only good things could come in the future. He would be the King of Kings. It was just a matter of time until He took the throne.

The Host had explained many things over the three years of their travels. His handpicked followers did not understand what spiritual events were playing out in front of their eyes. They simply accepted the invitation to dinner. They came. They partook. Spiritually, they were never the same.

Would you like a similar invitation? The Host is still inviting people to His table. You can arrive at any time and stay as long as you like. Your life will be forever changed.

Come. Partake of the Dinner of the Lamb.

The Last Supper

Before His arrest, trial, and crucifixion, Jesus started a tradition that Christians have continued throughout the centuries. He offered bread and wine to His disciples as they dined together that last evening. Thinking they were celebrating the Passover, a traditional Jewish celebration, Jesus' disciples did not fully understand His instructions. He simply told them to remember Him each time they ate together in the future.

Just as He told them to remember, He also tells each of us to remember Him. Never forget what He represents or what He did for us. Jesus Christ is the New Covenant provided by our Heavenly Father. Within the cup and bread offered at His Last Supper is the ultimate promise of the New Covenant, Jesus' blood sacrificed to save all mankind.

Believers still commemorate that evening, often calling it Communion. Most Christians have participated in Communion Services. This Holy Sacrament has been known by many names throughout history and is celebrated in various ways. Holy Communion, The Lord's Supper, The Eucharist, The Blessed Sacrament, The Meal that Heals, The Love Feast, The Marriage Supper of the Lamb, and The New Covenant are all names which indicate the celebration or remembrance of Jesus' Last Supper with His disciples.

Several other terms are closely related to communion, such as commune, common, community, communicate.

Commune can mean:

* eating together
* sharing with
* living with
* a group of people who live together sharing everything in common.

Communion indicates a feeling of relational or spiritual closeness. It involves sharing or communicating. It invokes a sense of shared religious identity, fellowship of ideas, or beliefs in common with each other. In fact, the word "common" indicates a shared belief or trait.

Communication and Community

Communication and community are also related. Communication is sharing information between entities. There are dozens of ways to communicate between people. In fact, every living thing has their own way to communicate if you understand their language.

5 different ways to communicate:

- Spoken word
- Written word
- Touch
- Actions
- Body language

A **community** is a certain group of people who live within a designated area. Examples would include a

- City
- Suburb
- Town
- Neighborhood

There also can be smaller communities (e.g. church or school) within a larger community.

The True Communion we are addressing encompasses all those concepts and analogies, yet also exceeds them all. It means an intimate relationship where something very personal and important is shared. The people of God (the community of believers in Jesus) come together to share (commune) with each other and with our Triune God. Just the act of coming together communicates belief in Jesus and the desire to share this very intimate experience; it is a common goal of celebration between every participant.

Amazingly, this growing community is not limited to a certain geographical region. The Christian community circles the earth. Can you even fathom the importance of the ever-expanding family of God sharing or communing at the Lord 's Table everywhere within the four corners of the earth?

Tradition Within Community

Since the Last Supper of our Lord some two thousand years ago, Christians have developed many ideas and traditions about the celebration of Communion. Some traditions teach that the liquid and bread are actually transformed into the blood and body of Jesus. Others teach that God is present in the drink and bread. Most contemporary Christians think the cup representing His blood and the bread representing His body transforms the believer as they partake of the elements of Communion, becoming one with Him in the Covenant of His blood.

What Happens During Communion?

Each person will describe something different. Some may feel total peace while others are overcome with emotion. Some may cry or laugh. Some may be totally and miraculously healed.

The power of God has no limits. Our God is a transforming God and He certainly can give supernatural signs to His people during Holy Communion. He delights in blessing His children.

One of our friends, Joshua Mills, has had some unusual manifestations of the Holy Spirit in his services. On a number of occasions while he was preaching, the water in his podium bottle became wine. He has had instances where oil flowed from his hands so profusely that he collected the overflow in bottles and sent them to his friends. We have used some of this remarkable oil in our anointing services.

Another friend in ministry has also experienced unique signs of God's supernatural presence in services. God often causes manna to appear on top of her open Bible when she is teaching. The manna is later used during Communion.

There are no limits to our God! It is possible for God to transform one thing into another or create something out of nothing if He chooses to do so.

Jesus said to the Jews,

> *"You think that because you are the sons of Abraham you are important. You boast about this and you think that means you're more valuable than other people, but I want you to know that my Father can turn rocks into sons of Abraham if he wants to."*
> *Matthew 3:9*

So can God do the miraculous? Yes. His miracles, signs, and wonders appear from unexpected directions and in various ways all the time. We know He will provide everything we need even though His miracles may slip silently into our world without bright lights, bells, or whistles announcing their arrival.

God can miraculously intervene at any time. Stay alert to the leading of the Holy Spirit no matter what you are currently experiencing. Expect Him to act! God isn't moved by pleading, begging, and crying. He is moved by faith. Even though

God can heal during Communion, He may not heal everyone who participates in this intimate remembrance of His suffering and death.

God is causing, directing, allowing, or guiding the events in your life for your benefit and His glory.

> *"And we know that all things work together for good to those who love God, to those who are the called according to His purpose." Romans 8:28*

If you are unaware of these truths, you need to pray that He will open the eyes of your understanding to the reality of the spiritual realm and your place in it.

> *"That the God of our Lord Jesus Christ, the Father of glory, may give to you the spirit of wisdom and revelation in the knowledge of Him, the eyes of your understanding being enlightened; that you may know what is the hope of His calling, what are the riches of the glory of His inheritance in the saints, and what is the exceeding greatness of His power toward us who believe, according to the working of His mighty power." Ephesians 1:17-19*

Unfortunately, it is possible to walk around and through the work of God and his angels on the earth and never recognize His Word. We are spiritual beings living in a physical, material world, but we must exercise our spiritual senses to understand the spiritual realm.

"No, we declare God's wisdom, a mystery that has been hidden and that God destined for our glory before time began. None of the rulers of this age understood it, for if they had, they would not have crucified the Lord of glory. However, as it is written: 'What no eye has seen, what no ear has heard, and what no human mind has conceived' the things God has prepared for those who love him— these are the things God has revealed to us by his Spirit." 1 Corinthians 2:7-10

Repeated often, we are a spirit, we have a soul and we live in a physical body. Our entire life span is within His spiritual realm whether we recognize Him or not. It is a believer's choice to walk in the physical or spiritual realm. Our physical life is temporary. Our spiritual life is eternal.

God is intimately involved with all aspects of life – from our first breath to our last. If we recognize His presence and give Him credit for all things, being aware of His presence is part of everyday life. Thinking about Him, talking to Him, feeling Him, hearing His voice becomes the ordinary, not the extraordinary.

Do this Often, the Remembrance of Him

Through times of intimate, regular Communion, remembering what Jesus has done for you increases your sensitivity to His presence and opens your spirit to His leading. You will know Him better, experience His miracles more often, and be willing and able to follow His instructions. You will walk in His footsteps. He will use your hands to reach out and touch with healing. He will speak words through you someone else is desperate to hear. In obedience, you become an earthly extension of your Father God.

For instance, the person you sit next to on a plane could be an angel. The person you bump into in a convenience store at midnight might be a special messenger from Him. That person who asks something inconvenient of you might be sent by God. If you are walking with God and living for God, there are no coincidences in your life. Through communing with Him, You will know His voice spoken through a child or a stranger. You will welcome and expect the favor of God in everyday occurrences.

Symbolism of Communion

The observance of the Lord's Supper, or Communion, contains the very seed of the gospel: all the symbolism of the life, death and resurrection of Jesus Christ. In Jesus, the ancient ritual of Judaic Passover observance was brought into the New Testament, updated as the Last Supper of our Lord. It was God's idea, not our own. Just as Jews still observe their deliverance from bondage with the Passover feast, we observe our deliverance from sin during Communion. Through Moses, God gave His people instructions on how to observe the Passover of the Old Covenant (Exodus 12:21- 28) and our Lord Jesus left the example of Communion for us to follow in His New Covenant (John 6: 48-58).

Whatever name you use—the Lord's Supper, the Love Feast, the Marriage Supper of the Lamb—Communion contains all the significant, divine elements of the gospel in one simple, beautiful ceremony. Since Jesus washed His disciple's feet during His last evening with them, some cultures even add foot washing to the intimate Communion celebration symbolizing the complete servanthood of Jesus as well as His Covenant.

Is Communion Necessary?

Man was created to be a companion, a friend of God. He wanted total communion with His creation. God didn't want to be separated from His most important creation. What can possibly separate a Holy, omnipotent God from His creation? Sin. God created us with a choice of following Him, or following the enemy. He knew man wasn't perfect. He knew He had to provide a way to reconcile imperfect man to a perfect God.

"And according to the law almost all things are purified with blood, and without shedding of blood there is no remission." Hebrews 9:22

The Bible tells us there is no forgiveness of sins without the shedding of blood. In the Garden of Eden, Adam and Eve sinned by doing the one thing God told them not to do. After confronting them with their sin, God led them out of the garden and clothed them in animal skins to hide their nakedness. God Himself killed the first animal as a blood sacrifice for their sin.

The Old Testament tells us the priests required people to bring a perfect animal as a sacrifice to atone for their sins. To be an acceptable sacrifice, the animal could not have any flaws. It had to be perfect. It had to be the best gift available.

The Ultimate Sacrifice

Farmers always save their best animals to develop quality herds for future income. The weakest animals are butchered while the best producers are carefully and wisely bred over and over again to maintain and increase the quality of a herd. Bringing the best animal to God in ancient times was truly a sacrifice. Giving away a valuable perfect specimen showed their faith in God's total provision. They willingly gave their best to atone for their sins as God required.

God desires to become one, to commune with His children. Reconciled, those who are born again move from strength to strength, faith to faith, and glory to glory as they are transformed by His glory. A sacrifice is always necessary to allow this union between God and man. It is a sacrifice that man can't ever provide alone.

Only Jesus could pay the price for sin. Only Jesus could become the ultimate sacrifice. Eventually, just as God provided the first sacrificial covering for Adam and Eve, He also provided Jesus, God in human form, as the last sacrifice to pay the price for the sins of mankind forever. He provided a perfect way through His perfect Son, Jesus Christ.

Can you imagine the conversation in heaven between God and His Son? "I love My children, but they just don't get the message of obedience to My laws. More and more sacrifices are brought but the people don't change. I need help. I need a perfect sacrifice, Jesus, which will take care of this problem once and forever."

Jesus simply said, "What can I do?"

God explained, "I don't want to be separated from My children. I must provide a perfect sacrifice to reconcile My children to Me. I want to send You down to earth as a human baby. You will grow and learn everything about living on earth as a man.

Eventually, You will reveal Yourself as My Son. One day You will lay down Your earthly life for every human being on earth. You will be the ultimate sacrifice for all time. All they have to do is recognize You as My Son and believe in Your sacrifice. They will be born-again into Your spiritual eternal body and with My Holy Spirit living inside of them, they can follow You and spread the Good News around the world."

A righteous, perfect Son of God replied, "Here I am. Send Me."

Today, believers are covered with the righteousness of Jesus Christ because of His blood sacrifice. Animal sacrifices were temporary, material, and had to be repeated year after year. Jesus' sacrifice is eternal and spiritual. Without His battered and bleeding body, you have no covering, no forgiveness, no reconciliation, no healing. Without Jesus' sacrificial death, you cannot be made whole. Without His shedding of blood, you have no salvation. All of mankind would be doomed to eternal damnation.

Jesus often spoke things to the Jews that they didn't understand or want to hear. One day He said to them,

> *"'I am the living bread which came down from heaven. If anyone eats of this bread, he will live forever; and the bread that I shall give is My flesh, which I shall give for the life of the world.' The Jews therefore quarreled among themselves, saying 'How can this Man give us His flesh to eat?' Then Jesus said to them, 'Most assuredly, I say to you, unless you eat the flesh of the Son of Man and drink His blood, you have no life in you. Whoever eats My flesh and drinks My blood has eternal life, and I will raise*

him up at the last day. For My flesh is food indeed,
and My blood is drink indeed. He who eats My flesh
and drinks My blood abides in Me, and I in him.
As the living Father sent Me, and I live because of
the Father, so he who feeds on Me will live because
of Me. This is the bread which came down from
heaven—not as your fathers ate the manna, and
are dead. He who eats this bread will live forever."'
John 6: 48-58

Jesus was saying to them, "Eat My body: become one with Me. Think My thoughts, hear My heart, commune and walk with Me."

God Made Man and Women

In Genesis, God put Adam asleep and took Eve from His side. When Adam woke up, he said to Eve,

"You are bone of My bone and flesh of My flesh."
Genesis 2:23

When Adam looked at Eve, he knew she was everything he ever wanted. He knew she was right for him because she had his nature. She was a feminine reflection of him. She was not someone randomly chosen by God just so Adam wouldn't be lonely any more.

Jesus Christ made His sacrifice so He could say to you, His bride, "You are bone of My bone and flesh of My flesh." The spear that pierced His side made a place for you in His heart for all eternity. When Jesus looks at you, He wants to see someone who has His DNA and reflects His nature. God intends for you to be that kind of bride for His Son. The Father sacrificed His only Son so Jesus would have a bride that looks like Him and reflects His image.

So long ago, His disciples gathered in the Upper Room to celebrate the Passover, a pivotal event in Jewish history. They had no idea what was about to happen would change the whole world.

> *Jesus said to them, "But I say to you, I will not drink*
> *of this fruit of the vine from now on until that*
> *day when I drink it new with you in My Father's*
> *kingdom." Matthew 26:29*

What He did not say aloud was, "This is the last time I do this. My final sacrifice is for everyone for all time and eternity. The next time we will share the Marriage Supper of the Lamb will be in heaven. The party that never ends will be for all those who eat My flesh and drink My blood."

No, He didn't mean anyone would actually cut up His body to eat it or collect His blood to drink it. However, He did mean we would have to accept and forever remember His ultimate sacrifice. All believers who willingly accept Jesus' sacrifice, believe in Him, and follow Him will be welcomed into His kingdom.

Nothing contaminated with sin can enter into God's presence. However, covered with His blood and as a member of His Body, God no longer sees our sin. He welcomes us with loving open arms.

Red Blood Shed on the Cross

+

Blackness of your Sin

=

Pure White Snow

Blood Covenant

The ceremony of Communion is a very Holy Sacrament of the Church. Indeed, it is a solemn remembrance of a very serious event; however, the result is not one of sadness or grief. Today, Communion reminds us that Jesus' sacrifice brings us New Life, reconciliation with our Heavenly Father, forgiveness of our sins, the Way to His joy, peace, happiness, and love. His Body and Blood cleanses us, makes us whole, takes away all sin, and allows us access into the throne room to visit our Father for the ultimate True Communion.

In addition to the blood sacrifices necessary to atone for sin, promises or agreements between two people were sealed in blood. For example, the co-mingling of their blood sealed the promise between David and Jonathan. (1 Samuel 18:3) The Old Covenant between God, Abraham, and his son Isaac was made through sacrifice. God supplied the animal for the sacrifice after Abraham was willing to sacrifice his son. (Genesis 15:17-18)

Blood is the life of the body. You can lose an arm or leg and still live. If blood is lost, life is gone. With Jesus' blood running through your body, you have His life in You. You can think like Him, you can act like Him, You can heal like He did. In the New Testament and through Communion, man receives the New Covenant from God through Jesus' blood sacrifice. The "drink" used during Communion will always signify His blood. It represents a Blood Covenant, which unites us with the Father, Son and Holy Ghost.

Why Do We Eat Bread?

Jesus is the Bread of Life. Without bread we starve, both physically and spiritually. In Bible times, bread was the main course, not a side dish. Bread was a necessary item for life. During the Lord's Last Supper, a ten-course meal wasn't served. Only bread and wine are mentioned.

Even the Children of Israel ate Manna, a form of bread, as sustenance for forty years. It was fresh every day, just as Jesus supplies us with new bread, a new word, a new Jesus every day. He gives us the opportunity to commune with Him through prayer, anywhere and anytime.

You have to willingly choose bread: the important thing. Eating enough bread nourishes and sustains life. Without bread, one starves spiritually.

True Communion is God's promise of eternal life where we will live forever in complete union with the Triune God, Father, Son and Holy Spirit. True Communion on earth is as close as we can get to heaven on earth.

Communion is about co-mingling His nature with ours. Are you ready? His invitation is waiting. Can you hear His knock at the door? Are you dressed and ready for Communion at the Lord's Table, at His Marriage Feast?

Ministering Communion

A Communion service can be done in many ways. Each can have a powerful effect on the participants; there is not one perfect way. In a small group, one or two people may pass the elements, the bread and cup. I've seen it administered by one person. I have seen it passed by the pastor and spouse to everyone. I have seen it performed by home group leaders and elders in a very powerful manner. I have been in many meetings where each person received a personal prophecy and was prayed over one by one. I've been in meetings where hands were laid on everyone for healing.

Even the position of your body cannot be dictated. Some want to sit. Occasionally people stand at the altar. And others will take the elements as they kneel.

Interestingly, when we were in Israel visiting the original Upper Room, our guide demonstrated the position most people took in Bible times. The famous picture of the Lord's Supper has everyone sitting on chairs on one side of a table. It is not exactly an honest portrayal. There were no "chairs" as we know them. The tables were low to the floor as people leaned on their elbows and used their fingers to eat the morsels of bread. People lounged or lay around the table, perhaps even leaning against one another.

There are many effective ways to administer Communion. Churches tend to do it only according to their accepted policies and procedures, but that is not necessary. On occasion, one church had groups of family members come to the table where the father, the head (priest) of the family, gave the bread and cup to each of his family members.

Some people take Communion daily at home or in their prayer closets. Some take the bread first; some take the cup first. Some use unleavened bread as in the Passover Meal; others use a loaf of bread broken in pieces, while others use crackers. The leader may dip the bread in the cup and place it in your mouth. Some allow you to dip and eat. Sometimes wine is used, sometimes juice.

Church policy may indicate passing the Communion plates of bread and cups throughout the congregation so everyone can drink and eat at the same time. Another denomination asks that everyone approach the altar and receive the elements of Communion individually. With the concern of spreading infection, the elements have even been prepackaged for single use. These can be opened readily at the right moment or easily carried to someone who is hospitalized or homebound.

Church policy may also dictate either open or closed Communion. Closed Communion is only available to those who meet certain criteria, usually membership in the denomination or church. Those groups who practice open Communion invite anyone who believes in Jesus and is saved to participate in the service and share the sacraments. We believe and practice open Communion. Whether you participate in a service is strictly between God and the individual.

Allow yourself to be creative. If you are going to be ministering Communion yourself, ask God what He wants you to do. I feel the more you honor Communion, the more you honor God and His great sacrifice of His only Son. If you participate in The Lord's Supper only once a year, I would question whether you really understand what Communion means to a believer's life. There are many traditions in Christianity, and different methods are used in administering this sacred sacrament. Ask God what He wants and obey Him. Do it with reverence. Do it joyfully and expect something good to happen.

Understand the Elements

Everything we do with Him has both natural and supernatural elements. The natural man focuses on the natural elements, but True Communion is also spiritual. Yes, many people have been healed during Communion. Many have been delivered of evil spirits. God is never limited to the natural means when we act in faith. No word God ever speaks returns void. Actions of obedience always produce a supernatural response from God. You don't know what He is going to say, and He usually doesn't explain what is going to happen.

His instructions may be brief and incomplete. He simply says, "I want you to do this" and then leaves it up to you to determine how to complete His assignment. However, if you act in obedience, something supernatural will occur. I've heard many testimonies over the years of His miracles occurring during Communion. In addition to physical healings, marriages have been put back together. There is no limit to what God can do if you act in faith and obedience.

How should we use Scripture in Communion? Study all the references to His final night. Understand what the Word says about True Communion. Jesus, the Word, instructed us to participate in Communion in remembrance of Him. Traditionally, we recall the stripes He experienced for our healing, the cross He carried to Golgotha down the Via Delarosa, the pain as they nailed Him to the tree, and His slow agonizing death as the ultimate sacrifice for the sins of all mankind.

The story of the Last Supper can always be shared if time permits and the principles are taught. Often, there is only a short time allowed for this special communion of believers. More in depth teaching can be done later. However, everyone needs to know and remember why Jesus invited His special friends to that first, but last, Supper before facing His accusers.

Remember

His love for us didn't stop at the Cross. It didn't cease as He arose victorious out of the tomb three days later. He promised His New Covenant was eternal. He spoke of joy, peace, and love to last forever. We can receive all His promises when we belong to His family. God is our loving Provider, our Father. Jesus is our brother, our Redeemer, and our Savior. No, His Love and Power did not stop at the Cross. His love multiplied across the world and through the centuries to the present, to you and me.

We continue to remember what Jesus did on the Cross; however, we also must remember what He has done for us this year, this month, today. The blessings that flow from the cross are continual and eternal. He provides all we need. What has He done for you this year? What did He do for you today?

In 2010, I had a knee that was painful to stand on. I prayed for hundreds of people to get new knees but mine seemed to be on "backorder." I couldn't stand on my knee, but I knew that I could stand on the Word. Even though I had to stand on His Word for an uncomfortable period of time, I knew if God was sending me all around the world to share His message, He would provide a new knee. He healed my knee. In my life, He has healed me of breast cancer and a broken back. He has healed me of a broken heart. Glory to God! He's healed me of dozens of things. I am a walking testimony of His healing power and love! God has met my every need and has blessed my children.

These are just a few of the things I remember while receiving Communion. Each and every time I receive Communion, I will remember what He is currently doing for me. In addition to dying on the cross, or the stripes on His back, He has made provision for my healing. He was wounded for my transgressions and all of my heart issues so that I would be cleansed from sin and no longer have to experience pain.

These are some of the things He has done for you also. Consider His faithfulness to you that occurs on a daily basis. It is what He is doing now! Not just what He did over two thousand years ago, but also what He is doing in your life today.

Communion is sacred. It is holy. It symbolizes the union of God with man. After today, I hope and pray you will never again participate in the Lord's Supper with a casual attitude. Preparing your heart for Communion is very important.

"For as often as you eat this bread and drink this cup, you proclaim the Lord's death till He comes. Therefore whoever eats this bread or drinks this cup of the Lord in an unworthy manner will be guilty of the body and blood of the Lord. But let a man examine himself, and so let him eat of the bread and drink of the cup. For he who eats and drinks in an unworthy manner eats and drinks judgment to himself, not discerning the Lord's body. For this reason many are weak and sick among you, and many sleep." 1 Corinthians 11:26-30

Never take Communion with a casual attitude. Prepare yourself. Sharing Communion can change your life. It will invite miracles into your life. Communion draws you closer and closer to the One who created you, who loves you like no other. Eating His Word, drinking His lifeblood, and allowing Christ to live within you will usher you into the Holy of Holies. You will experience True Communion with the King of Kings and the Lord of Lords. You will experience heaven on earth and see through His eyes. You will love with His love, and truly walk with God into eternity.

His invitation to dinner arrives daily. Receive His Word. Open His invitation. Commune with the Lord Jesus Christ; do not forget His great sacrifice. Partake of His Body and His Blood. Be One with Him. Be His hands and feet. Be His mouthpiece to bring others to His Holy table. Be an extension of the One Who gave it all just for you.

Join the Family at the table. Your Host is waiting with outstretched arms to welcome you home.

Preparation

The time of preparation will show your value, and honor of the Communion celebration.

- Estimate how many people will participate.
- Read the Scriptures about what was done and said on the night that Jesus was betrayed.
- Prepare your heart so you can lead others to the table.
- Let God lead you as you plan what you will say during the service.
- Pray:
  - "The Body of Christ, given for you. The Blood of Christ, shed for you."

- Quote a passage from Scripture that quotes Jesus' words.
- Listen to God's voice and obey.

- Prepare the environment:
  - Create a quiet, private, comfortable, intimate, and welcoming place.
  - It doesn't matter if it is indoors or outdoors.
  - Soft music will set the mood and discourage loud, disruptive talking.
  - Some will want to pray before, some after.

- Bread:
  - Any type of bread can be used: unleavened, crackers, homemade or store bought. Communion wafers obtained at the Christian bookstore are convenient, but not necessary.
  - Break bread into small pieces that are easy to pick up with fingers.
  - Use an attractive, clean plate or tray, perhaps with a napkin between the plate and bread.

- Drink:
  - Decide what will be served: wine or grape juice.
  - Small cups can be obtained at the Christian bookstore, but any small containers work just as well.
  - Fill the cups prior to service for better time management; you will also reduce the risk of spilling. However, for a small group, pouring from a small pitcher can work just as well.

- Miscellaneous:
  - Have a prayer partner—Both to pray before, during, and after the service.
  - Napkins, tissues and paper towels on hand. People spill things so be prepared. Some may cry. Again, be prepared.
  - Keep a waste basket nearby for the used cups, tissues, or discarded trash.
  - Set up a table to hold all the Communion elements.
  - Provide comfortable places to sit, lay, kneel, or lounge.

Foot Washing

5

IN JOHN CHAPTER 13, Jesus washed the feet of His disciples just before He was arrested, beaten and crucified. Many Christians have taken His example to minister to each other in a way that is powerful and unifying.

Foot washing acts are often a part of ordination or installation ceremonies for deacons, elders, missionaries or pastors, but they can also be conducted among any group of believers, even a husband and wife. Most are conducted for an individual or a small group of people, although it can be done in front of a larger congregation.

One of the most powerful revelations I have heard about foot washing and its significance is in the symbolism of what is represented. When Jesus walked the earth, all they had for transportation was their feet, donkeys, or horses. There was no mass transportation. Their ability for getting to where they needed to go was mostly connected to their willingness to walk there. Washing another person's feet in Biblical times represented the importance of removing the dirt from their travels. Cleaning the dust and dirt from the long journey meant that whatever their past, it was now completely washed away. The focus was brought to the purpose at hand, not the journey that brought them to that place.

Traditionally we are taught that Jesus and the disciples wore sandals. Obviously, there were not tennis shoes or boots. Their feet were constantly exposed to the elements; washing the feet and participating in the washing of feet ceremony meant that you were washing away unwanted dirt. This represents leaving the past and choosing to walk into your future.

One day God led me to wash all of my employee's feet. I brought a pillow for me to kneel on and I had a basin for each one of them. I washed their feet and told them how much I appreciated them and *all* they do for this ministry and me. I prophesied over many of them. It was one of the most moving times we have ever had as a team.

For some, they cried. For others, they were moved within their spirit, and within the team a greater sense of unity was created.

This ceremony is sometimes accompanied by a teaching on the life of Jesus Christ. His life's work is generally presented as a life of sacrifice and service to others using John 13 as the text.

> *"After that, He poured water into a basin and began to wash the disciples' feet, and to wipe them with the towel with which He was girded. Then He came to Simon Peter. And Peter said to Him, 'Lord, are You washing my feet?' Jesus answered and said to him, 'What I am doing you do not understand now, but you will know after this.' Peter said to Him, 'You shall never wash my feet!' Jesus answered him, 'If I do not wash you, you have no part with Me.' Simon*

Peter said to Him, 'Lord, not my feet only, but also my hands and my head!'" John 13: 1-5

"Now that I, your Lord and Teacher, have washed your feet, you also should wash one another's feet."
John 13:14

Foot Washing Ceremony Supplies

You will need:

- A large, plastic basin or tub for water for each person participating in the foot washing. (Do not use the same water for different people receiving the foot washing. Do not use too much soap in the water. It will leave a residue on the skin and can be irritating to the people participating in the foot washing.)
- A chair for each person participating in the foot washing.
- A pitcher used for filling the basins or tubs.
- A gentle, hypoallergenic soap or hypoallergenic foot soaking lotion.
- A large towel for underneath the basin or tub.
- A large towel for the person's feet after the ceremony.
- Box of tissues. (Depending on how many people are participating in the foot washing ceremony, you will want to have boxes spread throughout the group. It is a very humbling experience to receive this act of service from an employer, spouse, friend or pastor.)

- Light soaking music or instrumental worship music is good for background and for creating the atmosphere for this ceremony. (It is not required, but recommended.)
- Always have more towels and tissues than what you think you will need. It is better to be over prepared than feel like you were not prepared.

Directions:

Place the towels on the ground for each person that is participating in the foot washing. Put a small amount of soap in each basin. Use the pitcher to fill each water basin with warm water. Be careful not to use water that is too hot, or to fill the basins with too much water. Remember, you want both feet to fit in the basin and the water to not overflow onto the floor beneath it. The towels below the basins are there for when they remove their feet from the basin, or if the basin gets knocked over for any reason. It is highly unlikely but it is still good to be prepared for the 'just in case' situations.

If you are doing the foot washing ceremony on more than one person, arrange the towels and basins in a circle with room for you to move from one person to the next, allowing a reasonable distance between you and any basins while going from person to person. You don't want to knock them over in the middle of the ceremony.

After you have arranged the towels with their basins, and have put in the soap and water, arrange the chairs around the basins. Adding the chairs last will help you to avoid moving around the chairs with the water pitcher and soap.

Have each person participating in the foot washing sit in a chair. Order does not matter. The Holy Spirit will guide you as to who should sit where, go first, and go last. If He does not impress upon you where people should sit, then let each one choose. Even with them choosing, you will see that the Holy Spirit was guiding them.

Opening the Foot Washing Ceremony

Father, we bless Your name. We thank You for bringing all of us together for this amazing time of ministry. I ask You to pour out Your Spirit on us. Let us feel your presence. May this time together honor You and give You glory, in Jesus' name, amen.

Foot Washing Begins

After praying, go to the first person and have them put their feet into the water. Gently lift one foot up and use your hand like a cup to pour water over their foot. Pray as God leads for that person. While praying, move the washed foot to outside the basin, and lift up the second foot over the water basin. Again, use your hand like a cup to rinse off their foot while praying for them.

As God directs and speaks to you, share a prophetic word or encouraging word while you are washing their feet. Even the simplest of sentences or phrases can be exactly what that person needed to hear.

Pray Over Each Participant

Father, I thank You for giving Your Holy Spirit to us. I ask You to bless _____ (fill in the name) as they go from here into the destiny that You have for them. I thank You that they will know the path that You have prepared for them, and as they move forward and walk with You daily, I ask You to confirm to them that they are living in Your perfect will. I speak life, health and wholeness over them. I ask that You continue to pour out Your Spirit on them and that it would overflow into every area of their life. In Jesus name, amen.

Ministry Event Guidelines

USE THIS SECTION TO CREATE A FORM with essential ministry event guidelines that you can send to host churches.

Tips

- It will save time to have the host church fill out the date and time of service when you are first making arrangements. It will also help you in planning any travel, advertisements, and service preparations.

- Having a contact person for your website is very beneficial. It is best to have a phone number and e-mail for the contact. Let them know that this information will be included on your website or advertisements.

- Establish an honorarium for different ministry events. Consider having "local" and "travel required" honorarium. Understand the time and effort for different ministry events will help you gauge your honorarium. If in doubt, consider calling a ministry like yours, in the same growth stage as yours and ask what different honorariums are for that particular ministry. Also consider asking your pastor or someone else in ministry with you. The Holy Spirit also helps to guide you in setting up financial costs.

- It is very important to discuss what your hosts would like the service to look like while you are there. Over communication is much better than irritation, awkwardness, or embarrassing moments caused by a lack of communication.

Form Information

Ministry Name
Ministry Address
Ministry Phone Number
Ministry Website

- A $_____ seed (deposit) toward two airline tickets and/or expenses is required to reserve the date agreed upon. The balance for the airline tickets, if any, will need to be paid before the meeting. As soon as we set a date your event will be placed on the _____ calendar website.

- Mail your check, payable to _____, with this signed form. You may also call our office, xxx-xxx-xxxx to make a credit card payment, or online by clicking the "Speaker Engagement" button.

- Your event is not finalized until your deposit is received by our office. This means that YOU COULD LOSE YOUR DATE if the deposit is not paid within 30 DAYS.

- The following items are required:
  - One hotel room per night of ministry

- Pick up and transportation to and from the airport
- One six-foot table for teaching materials and product
- Table Cloths for table and extra cloth to cover product during service and overnight
- Praise and worship team for all services with sound system
- Two greeters per service
- Two ushers for offering
- Volunteers to assist when the Holy Spirit touches people during prayer
- Sound system with knowledgeable sound person for all services
- Room temperature bottled water and a glass for _____ at podium
- List the event with all FREE advertising sources, including Christian community calendars, newspapers, radio and (if available) television advertising—interviews are welcome
- Private room for ministry team if available
- Discuss arrangements for receiving offerings and come to an agreement with the pastor or event coordinator (some hosting churches will receive their tithes and offerings and give guest ministers an honorarium)
- Establish an honorarium before making final agreements on speaking dates, ministry events, weddings, funerals, baptisms, etc.

Ministry Event Advertising

- From our database, a postcard mail out will be sent to advertise in your area.
- Your event will be listed on our website and in our monthly e-blast **after your event is confirmed.**

Please read, print, sign, and fax to our office.

I have read and agree with the event guidelines as shown above.

Signed:	Printed:
Location Name:	Tentative Event Date:
Pastor's Name:	Location Website:
Address:	Phone:
E-mail:	Date:
Contact Name:	Contact Phone:
Contact E-mail:	

Service Date:	Time:
Service Date:	Time
Service Date:	Time:
Service Date:	Time:

**Please fax signed form to: Your Name Here
Fax Number and E-mail**

Receiving Offerings for Your Ministry

7

MANY PEOPLE FEEL AWKWARD about receiving of-ferings for themselves or their ministry. I have heard, "I will NEVER ask for money for me or my ministry." First of all, renounce those words, because you will need to do that in your ministry.

The Bible talks about money, blessings, giving, tithing, etc. More than it does about love. Obviously this is very important to God, so much so, He has it throughout the entire Bible.

A pastor and friend of mine told me when I was speaking at her church that they do not *take* offerings. They *receive* offerings. At first it hit me in a bad way. Now it bothers me when I hear "take." I thought about what she said. The more I thought about it, the more I agreed with her. I don't want to "take anything from anyone. I will be happy to "receive" any gift they want to give to God.

It is very important that YOU believe in YOU and what God is doing through you. When you do this, it is so much easier to receive offerings. It is important to give scriptural background as you are talking about giving. Add personal testimonies of what giving has meant to you, or share a recent financial miracle in your own life, and then one of a friend or partner. Sharing experiences of supernatural provision and blessings encourages other people to believe that God will supply their needs as well.

Receiving offerings and receiving people's criticisms as to how I "could do it better" is not always a fun situation. At first, this was very hard for me to get over. Some will complain that you took too long, while others will complain that you didn't talk long enough. Just remember, share what God has put on your heart and let Him speak to those who are to give into your ministry.

It is God's nature to be generous; those who reflect His character will also be giving people. A selfish, self-centered life is not possible in Christ. He gave all He had for us; we give because His love for us leads us to do so. Religious duty is not the motive for giving to God, and greed is not the motive for receiving offerings.

Giving tithes and offerings should be a joyous time when the children of God return a portion of what He has given them. It is also God's way to prove His involvement in the material affairs of His children. He provides for those who respond in faith to His love and give tithes and offerings. He not only can multiply whatever is left over, He also can bring in finances from many unknown sources. God's provision is miraculous and it is always there for those who learn to trust Him.

Tithing existed before Moses wrote the law. Everything we have comes from God. He asks us to honor Him by returning at least 10 percent to Him.

"Bring all of the tithe into the storehouse, that there
might be food in my house, and try me in this. If I
will not throw open the windows of heaven and
pour out such a blessing that there will not be room
enough to contain it." Malachi 3:10

Not being able to contain the blessings that God wants to pour out is a major benefit to obedience in giving the tithe and the offering.

It is necessary to teach on the importance of the offering. Deuteronomy 28 is a great Biblical text for receiving offerings. It shows the urgency of obedience and reveals the blessings of heaven received through obedience. It also follows with the curses of disobedience.

I remember one of the first offerings a friend received for a local ministry. She was asked to share her own giving testimonies and what God had done through her obedience in giving of offerings. She got very nervous and overwhelmed at the thought of receiving an offering. She later told me about the encounter she had with the Holy Spirit because of this situation.

She had become very nervous. Even when writing out her notes she thought to herself, *What if no one gives in this offering? What if this is the worst offering in the history of this ministry? What if this is the first and the last or only offering I'm every allowed to receive?* The Holy Spirit quickly spoke to her, "All you need to do is say what I am telling you to say. All you need to do is teach what you believe and receive the offering given. It is their responsibility to be obedient."

From that moment on, she was completely at peace and knew what she needed to do and say. That night she taught a great word, received the offering, and has received several offerings for her own ministry. She has become a great teacher and is no longer afraid to receive offerings because she knows how God blesses the obedience of His people.

Offerings and giving are not a heavy burden, but a happy opportunity. We belong to Him and it should be our joy to bless and honor Him in all things. We are even encouraged to be cheerful givers!

Encourage those that are giving to attach a Scripture to their offering or tithes. (It makes giving so much fun!) You cannot buy God's favor but you can plant a seed in faith and obedience. Watch God respond in miraculous ways. That is why we often suggest believers give with Philippians 4:19 in mind. When you give $4.19 (or $41.90 or $419), you are acknowledging that God's riches in glory are your source in Christ Jesus. He is our provider. The Bible is full of proclamations that can be used as a springboard for faith in giving. All we need to do is trust Him and give in harmony with His eternal Word. He will act to provide for us as we act in faith by giving.

Preparations for Receiving Offerings

After teaching on the importance of giving, pray over those attending the service. This should be a prayer from your own heart. In the end you can pray and speak a blessing over the offering.

Prayer Over Offering

Father I thank you for speaking to each one, their part in this offering. I thank you, because you have spoken and we receive this offering on Your behalf and for Your Glory. Thank you for multiplying their gifts supernaturally and honoring Your Word and their obedience. Amen.

- Have ushers or volunteers hand out offering envelopes.

- Tell those that are giving the monetary form of giving options that they have (cash, cheque or credit card).

- If they are giving by credit card, have a place for the three or four security code on your envelope. Having that code or the CVV# will save you a percentage on every donation given by credit card.

- For those who are writing checks, make them out to: (insert your ministry name or DBA.)

- Be sure to have a 501(c)(3) status in order to write tax receipts at the very beginning of every year. All donations must have an envelope to match them and have proper accounting done with them.

- Every donation given with a name and address will need to be recorded in a form of database. Cash given without a name, address or email address can be recorded as "public offering" and still requires accurate accounting of donations.

- Have an offering song selected and the music ready at the sound board. Be sure to discuss timing of playing the song, the volume of the song, and muting your microphone (if needed) after the song has started.

- Sometimes it is easier for a recorded song to be played than to have a full band come to the platform. A recorded song has a set time with no difficulty of people returning to the platform to play. Being familiar with the recorded song, you will know how much time you have to sit down or drink some water. One benefit of a live band is that if needed, the song can be played multiple times and people will not notice the length of the song. It is up to you and your hosts to decide.

- Do not make announcements during this part of the service. Most people are praying and or writing their information on an envelope and you will not have their full attention. Important announcements should be made at a separate time.

Receiving the Offering

After a couple of minutes, when you feel that there has been enough time for people to pray and hear God how much they are to give:

- Motion to the usher or volunteers that it is now okay to receive the offering.
- Have a basket for the offerings.
- Have them pass the basket down each aisle starting from the front.
- Some churches have the baskets at the front on the platform or altar. This allows people to give when they are ready and is a great option if you are short on volunteers or ushers. (Allow more time when the offering is brought forward. Realize that people have to get up from their seat and move around other people and chairs in order to get to the front. They

will also need time to get back to their seat without feeling like they took too long.

- Always thank those that are there for coming and supporting your ministry.
- It is great to share the needs the ministry has, as well as give the opportunity to become monthly partners with your ministry.

After Receiving the Offering

After receiving the offering, and the ushers have gathered the baskets, have one person responsible for holding the offering until after the service. After the service is over and all ministry time is finished, the "work of the ministry" begins.

It is advisable and highly recommended to have at least two people work on the offering together. Obviously, these people must be people of high moral and ethical standards. These are people that you are entrusting with the ability to help your ministry with their work. They can demolish it with their lack of integrity. It is very important to have trustworthy and honorable people help with your offering because it will affect your ministry in either a good way or bad way.

Be sure to document ALL cash, ALL checks and ALL credit card donations. Do not mix bookstore sales with donations in your accounting process. Mixing the two could create a disaster when it comes time for tax receipt letters to go out. It is very important and cannot be stressed enough: **MAINTAIN THE HIGHEST LEVEL OF ACCOUNTABILITY AND HONESTY IN ALL FINANCIAL MATTERS in your ministry as well as your personal finances.**

If you teach on the importance of giving make sure that you give too. Be a doer of the Word not just a teacher of the Word. Be a giver of offerings and be faithful in your tithe. Make sure that your ministry tithes, and gives offerings as well. It is not right to encourage others to do something, which you, yourself, are not already doing. Walk in the blessings of obedience just as you encourage others to do the same.

"Oh, taste and see that, the Lord is good! Blessed is the man who takes refuge in him! Oh, fear the Lord, you his saints, For those who fear him have no lack! The young lions suffer want and hunger; But those who seek the Lord lack no good thing."
Psalms 34: 8-19

8 Marriage Ceremony

THERE ARE MANY DIFFERENT styles and options for performing a wedding. The most important part of any wedding is getting to know your bride and groom before the service. Knowing how they would like the wedding ceremony to go beforehand is in your best interest. You may plan something out and while discussing it with the couple, may realize that particular style or choice of words does not suit them.

Remember to use this as an outline. There may be parts you really like and parts you don't. Remember to discuss all aspects of the wedding ceremony with the bride and groom. Take notes and listen carefully to what they are asking for, in any doubt, ask again. Every bride and groom would rather answer a lot of questions about the layout or specific design of their wedding, then to walk down the aisle after saying *I do* thinking *What was that?*

What we have done in this next section is give you a general layout of a service. In different sections within the marriage ceremony you have several options for phrases. Keep in mind this is only an outline; use small sticky notes, or write in pencil, words or phrases that you find to be perfect for such an important day.

In preparation for ministry, and in premarital counseling with the intended bride and groom, it is highly recommend for each couple to go through a discussion of what they plan their life together to look like. It is important to discuss:

- Do you want to have children?
- How many children do you want to have?
- What is the ideal plan you have for each other and your lives together in the first year of marriage? The first five years? Ten years? Twenty years? And so on.
- What precautions are you going to take now, and continue to implement in your life, to make divorce an inconceivable concept?
- Under what conditions would divorce become an option?
- What are you going to do to make sure you don't have that as an option?
- Do you fully understand that the commitment you are making is a lifelong covenant? It is truly a "till death do us part" decision?
- What are your individual concepts of finances and how to steward finances?
- What is your mindset regarding debt? (Is either one of you in debt? What is your agreed upon plan of action regarding your debt?)
- What are your financial goals as a couple?
- Who is responsible, once you are married, to balance the checkbook and pay the bills?
- Where do you plan to live once you are married?

- How do your families feel about you getting married?
- Have any family members mentioned concerns or reasons why you should not be married? Either now or in the future?
- Together, you need to discuss the boundaries of your sexual relationship and the expectations that you have toward one another. Making love is reserved for after the wedding ceremony, once you have fully committed to each other before God and man. (It may seem uncomfortable to ask about their potential sex life and their plans for finances but the top three reasons for divorce are: arguments about sex, financial management, and in-laws. It is a lot easier if you can help them create guidelines or agreements at the beginning of their relationship, rather than trying to unravel a train wreck two years into their marriage.
- Renounce any sexual covenants and take back any part of your heart that you may have previously given before.
- What do your plans as a married couple look like for Thanksgiving and Christmas? Discuss options of whose household you will spend holidays with, and let each set of in-laws in on the planning. (This may seem like a tiny detail but clear communication is key in avoiding unmet expectations.)

The Definition of Counsel:

- Act of exchanging opinions and ideas
- Consultation

- Advice and guidance, especially as solicited from a knowledgeable person
- A plan of action

Understand you are not a licensed counselor unless you have had formal education. Premarital counseling is a commonly used term and is not something that you should take lightly. Divorce rates among Christians are too high. Doing your part in the premarital aspect of things can only help the couple move forward in the right direction.

The right direction may not always mean making it down the aisle together. Moving in the right direction means that the couple has committed to saying and staying "I do" or "I don't" with a lifelong commitment rather than seeing the option of "I tried."

Opening the Ceremony

God bless you and thank you all for coming.

We are gathered here today for one of the most sacred events in the world, the joining of two people's lives. These two people standing before you will become one, forever and ever. Marriage is not a thing we "try out" to see if it works, marriage is an eternal covenant that two people make with each other before God.

The marriage covenant is probably the most sacred covenant in the Bible outside of the covenant of salvation. God expects you to take your promise to each other very seriously. Consider your marriage a precious and valuable union. Hold your marriage as close as you hold your salvation.

Marriage can be the most exciting and life-giving experience in the world, or it can be miserable. Your marriage depends on how you look at it, how you approach it. As marriage matures and the honeymoon excitement fades, your partnership can grow cooler.

The words, "I love you" may not be said as often. Kisses may not be as passionate as those first ones were. The heart doesn't beat quite as fast as your love comes into the room. What do you do?

Marriage is not just peaches and cream floating on a cloud with cupid shooting cute heart shaped arrows over your heads. Marriage is life. Marriage is work. If you want a successful, happy, fulfilling marriage, you must make the choice to follow God's advice.

As the excitement of a new marriage cools off, look at each other and remember how you felt when you first said, "I do." Share the exciting details of the day of the proposal. The most important memory to hold onto forever is that moment when you decided you wanted to spend the rest of your lives together.

Marriage between man and woman is an earthly example of the marriage of Christ and His Church. He gave His life for His Bride. He became a servant to save her life and assure eternal happiness for her.

When a man and woman join in holy matrimony, they give up their selfish desires. They become as one person. Their interest is now for another. What can they do for the love of their life? How can they support each other, encourage each other? If one is unhappy and sad, the other will feel the same pain.

The groom will have a lifetime to study his sweet beautiful bride. How can he help her, guide her, make her smile? The bride will likewise study how to make her spouse happy, content, and the best he can be. Helping each other, caring for each other, is a choice to be a servant to each other.

Love is a choice. Staying in love is a choice. Being happy together is a choice. Thank God every day for the spouse He has brought into your life. Praise Him for the love He has given you for each other. Don't try to change each other. Believe God to make the changes—so each is more like Jesus every day of the marriage forever.

Placement of Participants and Extended Family in the Ceremony

Traditional:

- Groom's side of the family is on the right.
- Bride's side of the family is on the left.
- Bride and her bridesmaids stand to the left side of the altar.
- Groom and groomsmen stand to the right side of the altar.
- Grandmother's are escorted in by ushers.
- Both bride and groom mother's are escorted in to light a unity candle.
- Both mother's are escorted to their seats, close to the grandparents.
- Pastor, groom, best man and groomsmen enter and take their place on platform.
- Bridesmaids enter in a single file line ending with maid of honor, matron of honor if she is married.
- Flower girl and ring bearer enter and take their place.

(If they are children, it is best to have them enter and then sit close to the family and not require them to stand for the duration of the wedding. They tend to draw attention and focus away from the bride and groom.)

- Bride enters and officiate motions for those attending the wedding to stand, sometimes led by the mother of the bride standing first.
- Discuss with the bride and groom: traditionally the bride and groom face away from their guests, facing the officiate. Consider the officiate facing the bride and groom with his back to the audience. It would in turn, have the bride and groom facing their family members, friends, and cameras.

Giving of the Bride

To the father OR family member representing or in place of the Father:

- Who gives this woman to be married to this man?
- Who gives this bride away?
- Who gives this bride to be with this groom?
- Who gives this woman to be with this man?

Response:

- Her mother and I do.
- We do.
- Our family does.
- With love and blessings, I do.

To the groom:

- Receive your bride and step forward with her.
- Take your bride and step forward.
- Receive your bride and join me here.

Charge to the Bride and Groom

If you will follow the "Be Attitudes" you will discover that they are the ingredients for the perfect marriage. Here are some "Be Attitudes."

- Be honest
- Be loving
- Be a best friend forever
- Be patient
- Be courteous
- Be considerate
- Be fun to live with
- Be desirous
- Be forgiving
- Be loyal
- Be one
- Be married
- Be in harmony with God's plan
- Be together in sickness and in health, for better or for worse, in the good times and the bad

If you had to choose one person to live with for the rest of your life, would you choose yourself? Standing here today, you are choosing in front of family and friends to live with each other no matter what, come what may.

"If you love someone, you will be loyal to him no matter what the cost. You will always believe in him, always expect the best of him and always stand your ground in defending him." 1 Corinthians 13:7

Marriage is something that is entered into only after considerable thought and reflection. It has many cycles, some couples have ups and downs, some couples have trials and tribulations, but God did not intend marriage to be a conflict. He wants you joyfully united. Jesus said, "I have come that your cup of joy might be full."

Ephesians 5:21-33 states,

"Submit to one another out of reverence for Christ. Wives, submit yourselves to your own husbands as you do to the Lord. For the husband is the head of the wife as Christ is the head of the church, his body, of which He is the Savior. Now as the church submits to Christ, so also wives should submit to their husbands in everything. Husbands, love your wives, just as Christ loved the church and gave himself up for her to make her holy, cleansing her by the washing with water through the word, and to present her to himself as a radiant church, without stain or wrinkle or any other blemish, being holy and blameless. In this same way, husbands ought to love their wives as their own bodies. He who loves his wife loves himself. After all, no one ever

hated their own body, but they feed and care for
their body, just as Christ does the church, for we are
members of His body. 'For this reason a man will
leave his father and mother and be united to his
wife, and the two will become one flesh.' This is a
profound mystery—but I am talking about Christ
and the church. However, each one of you also must
love his wife as he loves himself, and the wife must
respect her husband."

Sharing of Vows

To Groom:

_____, do you take _____ as your
wife? Do you promise to love her, protect her, cherish her, provide for her and honor her just as Christ does the Church?

Groom:

I do.

To Groom:

Turn to her and make this confession of your faith. Repeat
after me:

I, _____, according to the Word of God, leave
my father and mother and join myself to you. From this moment
on, we are one. I choose this day to give you my whole heart.

To Bride:

_____, do you take _____ as your
husband, submitting yourself to him as unto the Lord? Show-

ing and giving him honor, trust, and respect as the head of this union, family and future for the rest of your lives?

Bride:

I do.

To Bride:

Turn to him and make this confession of faith. Repeat after me.

I, _____, according to the Word of God, leave my father and mother and join myself to you. From this moment on, we are one. I choose this day to give you my whole heart.

Presentation of the Rings

To the Ring Bearer (OR to the best man and maid of honor):

May I have the rings please?

(Rings are given to the Officiate)

A ring is a very special thing. A ring on your finger indicates to the world your love for that one special person in your life. A ring is a significant symbol of love because it is an unending circle, it represents how your love goes on and on and never has an end. Wearing these rings should be a continual reminder of the favor you have found with God, as well as your commitment to each other.

To the Groom:

Take this ring and place it on her finger.

Officiate:

Repeat after me: With this ring, I thee wed.

Groom:

With this ring, I thee wed.

Officiate:

I give you this ring as a sign of my faith, hope and love.

Groom:

I give you this ring as a sign of my faith, hope and love.

Officiate:

May He bind our hearts and lives together forever.

Groom:

May He bind our hearts and lives together forever.

To the Bride:

Take this ring and place it on his finger.

A ring can mean two different things. It can be a decorative object that you wear on your hand. It can be a beautiful piece of jewelry that draws attention and gets compliments. Above all things, it should remain a sign and symbol of love that is shared between the two of you.

Officiate:

Repeat after me: With this ring, I thee wed.

Bride:

With this ring, I thee wed.

Officiate:

I give you this ring as a sign of my faith, hope, and love.

Bride:

I give you this ring as a sign of my faith, hope, and love.

Officiate:

May He bind our hearts and lives together forever.

Bride:

May He bind our hearts and lives together forever.

Personal Vows

An option that some couples really enjoy is sharing vows that they have written to each other. (If the bride and groom have decided beforehand or spur of the moment to share personal or self-written vows, let them do so here. If they have written them out beforehand, the maid of honor and best man can give them to the officiate before the start of the ceremony.)

Lighting the Unity Candle, Communion, or Unity Sand Ceremony

If the couple decides to have a unity candle, then they would go from saying their vows to the Unity Candle. Lifting their individual candles at the same time, they hold the flames together to light their unity candle. Then together, they blow out their individual candles.

Communion can also be shared during this part of the wedding. For the bride and the groom, the officiate would direct them through the elements of Communion.

The unity sand ceremony is a newer, trendier idea toward a unity ceremony. The bride and groom have a sand vase with their own choice of colored sand. Together they pour into a larger decorative vase, each pouring a little at a time till their sand vase is empty. It is a great symbolism of their relationship and how they are now inseparable.

A Marriage Blessing

"May the Lord bless you and keep you. May the Lord make his face to shine upon you, and be gracious to you. May the Lord lift up his countenance upon you, and give you peace."
Numbers 6:24-26

Make a God choice today, and every day, from this day forward. Make your marriage exciting! Read the Song of Solomon together. It is God's scriptural example of a wonderful man and woman relationship.

You have chosen each other above all others to love and cherish for the rest of your life.

As a husband and wife, a representation of God's love for the world, and Jesus' love for the Church, I encourage you to apply these simple sounding, sometimes difficult, words of advice:

- Never go to bed mad at each other.
- Remember to say "I love you" as often as you can.
- Learn to communicate in each other's love language.

- Be quick to forgive.
- Remember that marriage is a daily choice to submit and honor each other.
- Divide the household chores. Caring for a home or family is a partnership to share.
- Don't expect the other one to carry the full responsibility of making the marriage successful.
- Live as unselfishly as you can.
- Make God first in your life, and make sure that neither of you are first in your own life.
- Have common goals and discuss plans to reach those goals together.
- Pray together everyday.
- Study His Word together.
- Go to church together.
- Worship Him together in your home.
- Learn the importance of compromise when an easy agreement is not attainable.
- Remember to do what Jesus would do.
- Remember God is the One who brought you together; He can keep you together as long as you seek Him and His will for your lives and your family.

Officiate to the Audience

This couple has professed their love to each other and to God, and I want to give you the opportunity to do the same.

For this couple, a relationship with God is what drew the two of them together. They know that a person who stands alone is easily defeated. Two can fight back to back and save the other, but a three-strand cord is not easily broken. They know that the head of their house must be God in order for them to make it in this world.

For those of you who have once had a relationship with God or for those of you who have never known God, I want to invite you to join me in this prayer.

Repeat after me: Father, I have sinned. I repent for these sins. Take them from me now and put it on the cross, never to be held against me again. Jesus, I believe that You lived and died for my sins. Come into my heart and be Lord of my life. Thank You for guiding and directing me through Your Holy Spirit. Teach me to live like You and walk with You all the rest of my days. In Jesus Name, amen.

Prayer of Blessing Over Newlyweds

Father, in the name of Jesus, I speak a supernatural hedge of protection around this couple and their household. Father, I thank You that as they have chosen to spend the rest of their lives together, that they will also choose to glorify You in each moment that they share with each other. Let them be a beacon of light in a dark work and an example of a godly couple living for each other and giving You the glory. In Jesus' name, amen.

Officiate Announces Couple

_____ and _____ are so thankful that you could be here today to witness the start of their new life together.

Allow me to be the first to introduce you to Mr. and Mrs. (his first name) _____ (the couples agreed upon last name, if hyphenated) _____.

To the Groom:

_____, you may kiss your bride.

(Bride and groom kiss and then walk down the aisle together. The bridal party and immediate family members go down the aisle as practiced in the wedding rehearsal.)

Officiate:

Dismiss the friends and family that have come for this wedding.

Renewing
Marital Vows

Most Christian groups recognize the importance of marriage, and do whatever they can to strengthen marital unions. One way to accomplish this is through a ceremony of renewal. The minister will lead the married couples in a series of declarations similar to their original vows that reaffirm their commitment to each other before the body of Christ, in the sight of God. Unfortunately, our modern culture does not value long-term commitments and marriage is often seen as a temporary convenience that can be put aside at will. God does not view marriage this way, but rather as a reflection of Christ's relationship with His church.

The minister normally gives a message about the nature of marriage and leads the couples in statements of commitment before the whole congregation. These statements often have biblical references and may encompass children and family members.

Some like to dress up in a wedding dress or tuxedo or a nice dress and suit. Usually there is a maid (matron) of honor and a best man. Often people enjoy a big cake, or a dinner for close friends. Some NEED to renew their vows after a hard time in their marriage. Some just want to because of where they are in life. For example, I renewed one couple's vows on the Sea of Galilee, and another couple on the beach of Hawaii. Anywhere that might be special to them is a great place for a special ceremony.

The vows would be very similar to the actual wedding vows. Father, bless them!

10

House Dedication

For a Married Couple

BUYING A HOUSE OR MOVING into a new home can be traumatic for some people. For others, it can be a great source of excitement. Leaving the old and moving into the new can be overwhelming for some people. So if this was a hard move or a traumatic experience, put your hands on your heart.

Father, in the name of Jesus, I command any trauma or stress that came in from this move or purchase to be completely gone. Father, I thank You for your abundant peace falling on them. I thank You that any effect of stress and trauma will be completely gone in Jesus name. Amen.

A house is a wonderful thing. Any house can become a home where married couples become a family. It's where they can grow to love each other and see their family become all that God has called them to be. A house is more than just a place to keep your things. It is the place you can grow old together in, feel safe in, create life in and thrive in. It's where you can move forward into all that God has called you to do together. That is part of what you declare here today. Together you have decided to dedicate this home to the Lord and I honor you for that.

"As for me and my house, we will serve the Lord."
Joshua 24:15

It is important to not get caught up in the material things, the fine furnishings, or how much money you can spend. Stay focused on what God has called you to do. Remember that you can have the things of this world, as long as the things of this world don't have you. Do not let this house become a ball and chain around you or a divisive strength between you and your family. Remember to use all that you have been entrusted with to glorify God. It is very important to keep your priorities in alignment and to be faithful with what God has given you. This house is a gift from God, and by dedicating it to Him for His use and His glory, you are giving it back to Him.

So today, as you choose to dedicate this house to the Lord, for the use of His will, His work here on earth, the development of your marriage and family, and the growth your individual ministry, I urge you to keep this at the forefront of your mind: that today and from this moment on, "Me and my house, we will serve the Lord."

Prayer of Dedication

Father, we choose this day to honor You with this house and we give it back to You. We know that you have given us this house, entrusted us with this house, for Your glory. So father, we dedicate this house to You. We promise to stand firm as a united family, to serve each other in love, to be a safe haven for those in need, and to be a place of refuge from the storms of life.

Father, I thank You, that any thing that is not of You is gone in the name of Jesus. I speak peace, life, health, and wholeness into this house and all that enter here. I thank You for pouring out your Spirit in a fresh way in Jesus' name.

Father, we thank You for your abundant blessings, favor, and supernatural provision. Thank You giving us the ability to be a blessing to others. I speak a supernatural blessing over this home and this family, in Jesus name, amen.

For a Single Person, Single Parent, or Roommate

BUYING A HOUSE OR MOVING into a new home can be traumatic for some, but for others it can be a great source of excitement. Leaving the old and moving into the new can be overwhelming for some people. So if this was a hard move or a traumatic experience, put your hands on your heart.

Father, in the name of Jesus, I command any trauma or stress that came in from this move or purchase to be completely gone. Father, I thank You for your abundant peace falling on them. I thank You that any effect of stress and trauma will be completely gone in Jesus name. Amen.

A house is a wonderful thing. Any house can become a home when you have chosen to start a new phase of your life. It's where you can grow and mature in the Lord and become all that God has called you to be. A house is more than just a place to keep your things. It is the place you can feel safe. It's your refuge from the world and work environment; in it you create life and thrive.

You are moving forward into all that God has called you to do, and my prayer is that this house is part of you fulfilling your destiny. That is part of what you declare here today. You have decided to dedicate this home to the Lord and I honor you for that.

"As for me and my house, we will serve the Lord."
Joshua 24:15

It is important to not get caught up in the material things, the fine furnishings, or how much money you can spend. Stay focused on what God has called you to do. Remember you can have the things of this world, as long as the things of this world don't have you. Do not let this house become a ball and chain around you, but use it as an additional tool of ministry that you can use to bless others. Remember to use all that you have been entrusted with to glorify God. It is very important to keep your priorities in alignment and to be faithful with what God has given you. This house is a gift from God, and by dedicating it to Him for His use and His glory, you are giving it back to Him.

So today, as you choose to dedicate this house to the Lord, for the use of His will and His work here on earth, I urge you to keep this at the forefront of your mind: that today and from this moment on, "Me and my house, we will serve the Lord."

Prayer of Dedication

Father, we choose this day to honor You with this house and we give it back to You. We know that You have given (fill in name) this house and entrusted him or her with this house for Your glory. So father, we dedicate this house to You. We promise to stand firm on Your Word, to be a safe haven for those in need, and to be a place of refuge from the storms of life.

Father, I thank You, that any thing that is not of You is gone in the name of Jesus. I speak peace, life, health and wholeness into this house and all that enter here. I thank You for pouring out your Spirit in a fresh way in Jesus' name.

Father, we thank You for your abundant blessings, favor, and supernatural provision. Thank You for giving _____ (fill in name) the ability to be a blessing to others. I speak a supernatural blessing over this home and all who dwell here, in Jesus name, amen.

Baby Dedication

11

EACH CHILD THAT COMES into this world is a miracle of its own. We must always be thankful, and we must always welcome these babies into the world with loving arms. A wise person once said, "We do not go into our baby's world, but we welcome our baby into our world." I say that as a reminder.

Wives (mother's name), always remember, before you had your baby, you had your husband. He should always come first, and his space in your heart and life should never be replaced by the needs of your children.

Husbands (father's name), remember to love and embrace your wife, especially in front of your children. Children should never question the love and affection between their parents. Even when they make comments of "that's gross" or "get a room," it does more for their self-esteem and confidence than they will ever let you know. Your children should know by your words and actions that you love each other, are still thankful after years and years together, and that you still want to be with each other.

In the same way that you have asked God for your baby, we are going to ask Him to bless this child and the life that you have created together. This dedication is an act of worship to Him. Remember, He is the one who gave this child (these children). You have chosen to raise your child(ren) according to Biblical principles.

Prayer over the Child(ren)

Father, in the name of Jesus, I ask that You put Your angels around (baby's name). I ask that you would open this child's eyes to who You are and to reveal Yourself to them at an early age. I ask, as they grow older, that You would send friends to walk along side (baby's name) and encourage them in the destiny that You have placed inside him or her.

I speak supernatural clarity and direction over (baby's name). I pray that they will know the hope of their calling and walk in it all the days of their lives. Father, we give him or her to You, for Your purpose, Your will, and Your glory, in Jesus name, amen.

Charge and Prayer Over the Parents

A charge to the parents in this day and age can be hard to give and even harder to receive. I stand here today, with you, in this dedication ceremony to remind and encourage you that God has given you (baby's name) to raise. He has entrusted you with this life to shape and mold into a godly person.

Part of your responsibility in raising this child with Biblical principles, is to raise them to believe in God, love God, and be a voice in this world of the hope that we have through salvation. I ask you today to set aside any thoughts of befriending him or her. This charge is to remind you of the mandate and responsibility you have in shaping this baby into an adult. Remain their parents and you will gain friendship through this relationship built on honor and respect.

Father, I ask You to be the greatest source of strength, wisdom, and knowledge to (parents' names) these parents. I ask that You make their bond of marriage stronger and keep them unified, and in one accord, all the days of their lives. I ask that as they have dedicated their child to You, that we stand in agreement to dedicate them as parents to You.

Father, I thank You for giving them greater discernment and direction, both as a couple and as parents. I ask that You hold this family in Your arms and that You bless them in their walk with You. God, may they prosper and be in health, just as their soul prospers. Amen.

Charge and Prayer Over the Extended Family Friends

This can be the hardest part of a dedication: the charge to the family members (grandparents, aunts, uncles, etc.) that will help support the parents and be a voice of influence in this child's life (baby's name). You have an important role to fill. For some, you will be the person that (baby's name) turns to when they don't like the "no's" given to them by their parents.

The charge to you today is to take the same care and love that God has given to you, and freely give it to your family. Never be a voice of defiance or look to cause division. Always strive toward unity and peace; this is the charge to you today.

Closing Prayer

Father, I ask that You bless this family and the friends that are here with us today. I ask that You continue to reveal Yourself to them. We thank You for your grace and your mercy. We thank You for the salvation that we have through your Son, Jesus Christ. I ask that You guard our hearts and our lives and as we maintain our focus on You, that You would continue to bring clarity to every area of our lives. We ask all of this in Your name, amen.

Graduation

12

GRADUATIONS FROM high school, college, Bible school, etc., are happy occasions. Many believers see these as milestones to be celebrated and blessed. Every graduation opens the door to new opportunities. Graduates need to be encouraged to make good choices, as that in turn makes life-changing decisions. This is a good opportunity to engage a whole family with the gospel message who don't normally attend Christian services.

The attending minister usually crafts a message aimed at both the new graduate and others attending, particularly those not of the household of faith. It is common for gifts to be given to the graduates.

Father, we thank You for this monumental day in the life of _____. It has been many years in the making to get to this point. Father, I ask that You ordain _____'s steps in a greater way from this day forth. Anoint _____ and give him/her greater wisdom than ever before. Show them the right decisions to make.

"That the God of our Lord Jesus Christ, the Father of glory, may give to you the spirit of wisdom and revelation in the knowledge of Him, the eyes of your understanding, being enlightened; that you may know what is the hope of His calling, what are the riches of the glory of His inheritance in the saints, and what is the exceeding greatness of His power toward us who believe, according to the working of His mighty power." Ephesians 1:17-19

"'For I know the plans I have for you,' declares the LORD, 'plans to prosper you and not to harm you, plans to give you hope and a future.'" Jeremiah 29:11 NIV

Building Dedication

13

G OD IS INVOLVED in every aspect of our lives; whatever is important to us, is also important to Him. Our homes, businesses, and public buildings should all be used for accomplishing His will. As such we should not be ashamed to ask God to bless them. This is not superstition or magic, but simply a child of God asking for God's blessing on his home and work.

When you bless a building there are a number of different things you can do. I suggest you pray over the boundaries of the land, area, or building and dedicate it to God's glory. You will also want to ask God to protect all who come onto the property. It is usually customary to pray over the doors, windows and roads coming onto the property. Again, try to attach your faith to particular Scriptures that express your heart for that home, building, or land. It is common to use anointing oil on doorways and windows.

For older properties it may be wise to have a cleansing service. The owner may want to invite Christian friends over to pray the blood of Jesus over the building and anoint it with oil. Sometimes buildings have an atmosphere from previous owners that is not compatible with the Holy Spirit, but believers can change that through prayer and worship.

When we dedicated our land, we had a board member go to the four corners of the property. We all had our cell phones on speaker so we could all hear each other pray. We had several that spoke in different languages. We had them pray in Spanish from the southern corners (in the direction of Central America), as well as in English.

We took four HUGE nails (like used on the cross) and hammered them in the four corners of the property. Praying over that corner to the other corners. We prayed over any of the things of the past that had been done there that was NOT of God to be cleansed from it, and that the Spirit of God was going to wash over it and cleanse it.

> *"And after these things I saw four angels standing*
> *on the four corners of the earth, holding the four*
> *winds of the earth, that the wind should not blow*
> *on the earth, nor on the sea, nor on any tree."*
> *Revelation 1:7*

I got the name of this property and foundation a year or so before that day of prayer. Our Foundation is called "4 Corners Foundation." The area is known as "4 Corners." The property is in the northwest quadrant of the "4 corners." Then someone called us with this Scripture above.

Father, we thank You for blessing us (them) with this _____ (house, business, land, building). We dedicate it to You. We speak peace that passes ALL understanding. Thank You for using this _____ for Your Glory.

Many will come to know You here in this place and many will find refuge here. I thank You for the finances that You are going to bring into this _____ (business or family) and ideas on what they are to do here. (If a debt on it) Father, I thank You that You are going to show me how to pay it off. In Jesus' name. AMEN!

Funeral

14

YOU COULD ASK any pastor or minister and they would tell you, a funeral is never easy. What we are offering in the information to come is a guide to comforting the family members and friends that are here wondering why their loved one is gone. This is an outline of preparation and procedure in order to help you minister and start the healing process after losing a loved one.

As with anything in this book, become familiar with the information in it and use it as a guide in planning the funeral. A funeral will traditionally have a service with the casket at the front of the room. The family will decide if the casket is open or closed. For some it is less traumatic for it to be closed. It should also be discussed, if the evening before the funeral, if the family would like what is called a viewing, visitation, or wake.

The viewing, visitation, or wake is usually the night before the funeral. It is open for friends and family of the deceased to come for a more private time together. It is their time for showing respect to the other surviving family members and pay their last respects to the deceased as well.

There is also an option for the memorial service for those who want to be cremated instead of being buried. It is very important to know the family's preference and how they would like the service to go. If the deceased made prior arrangements, please honor them by fulfilling their last wishes.

Pre Service Checklist:

- Location for funeral or memorial service
- Time and date for service
- Flower arrangements and placements of family pictures
- Find out options for in lieu of flowers for those wanting to donate
- Family's plans for the service
- Bottled water for family members of the deceased
- Tissue boxes throughout the room where the service is being held
- Is there both a service at the funeral home or church as well as graveside?
- Light music playing in the background for when people are arriving
- Ask the family if any of them would like to share personal stories about the deceased
- Ask if the family would like one person to share or if they would like to open up the service to allow other people to share funny and light stories involving their loved one

- Ask them to considering making a video of pictures and film clips of their loved one, sharing their life from birth to recent life
- Ask if the family if the would like open or closed casket
- Ask them if they would prefer your help with the funeral director
- Help in coordinating seating arrangements at the funeral and graveside
- Prior to the day of the funeral, discuss the family's plan for the graveside service
- Help with coordinating a family with close friends for a meal after the graveside service (a dinner after the graveside can be arranged at your local church, the funeral home, family member's home or a friend's home. Help in covering the basics of a meal: plastic ware, napkins, cups, light snacks, main dish, fruits, etc.)
- Encourage a stable family member of the deceased to discuss costs of different services at the funeral home (those that are planning a funeral may feel like they didn't do enough while the family member was alive and may be inclined to overspend at the funeral in order to make up for it)
- Encourage a family to check other funeral homes to ensure that in their time of grieving and loss that they are not being taken advantage of

- Departure arrangements: whose cars will they be driving?
- Maps or service programs
- Coordinate removing family pictures and belongings from the funeral home
- Ask a family member or good friend to stay at the graveside until the casket is buried and the flowers have been placed over their loved one's plot
- Help to coordinate meals for the family a few days prior to the funeral and a couple of days following the funeral (to help with out of town guests and needs as well as make sure the family eats)

What to Say When You Don't Know What to Say

A funeral almost always has a great example of people who either say too much, or give a perfect opportunity for "open mouth, insert foot." It has been said:

> *"Empathy can in no way replace sympathy. What people need is sympathy." —Anonymous*

What to Say

- If you need anything, I am just a phone call away.
- I just want you to know that I really loved (fill in name) and they could never be replaced.
- The flowers are beautiful.
- I always loved that picture of him (or her).

- If you need anything in the next few weeks or help with the children, just let me know. I want to help you wherever I can.
- It was a beautiful service.
- I am glad your family was able to come in for the service.
- I am thankful (fill in name) was a great friend. I am thankful I had the opportunity to know him (or her).
- We love you and we're praying for you.
- When you're ready, I would like to plant a tree in his (or her) memory. (There are many great organizations such as charities, memorial funds, and non-profit organizations that receive donations in honor of a deceased loved one. Often the family will have a specific organization that they prefer. It is best to check with them when honoring someone's memory.)

As with anything that you say, do not say anything you do not mean. A great way to help someone in their greatest time of need is to look for where you could help them in their day-to-day life. The concept of "see a need, fill a need" applies greatly in this area. Oftentimes in overwhelming tragedies, or an unexpected loss of a loved that one, can be so traumatic that offering to help "wherever it is needed" may be intended to help but they will not call or e-mail the need that they have.

I have a friend who had a very traumatic event happen in their life and I offered to help wherever I could. It was over three months before she asked me to help. Not because she didn't need it, but she started realizing where she could really use help.

It is always so encouraging to see the body of Christ come together and love and serve those around them. Helping to coordinate meals the first few weeks after the loss of a family member can always help the grieving family. It is one less thing the parent or spouse will have to think about. It is a small act of kindness that alleviates a part of their "to do" list for the day.

I have seen other people step in and help families in different ways, along the lines of:

- I can watch your children while you run errands this weekend.
- I am going to the store right now. Want me to grab your family dinner while I am there? I can drop it off in about an hour.
- If you'd like, I can come and clean your house while the children are at school.
- If you'd like, I can help you around the house this weekend.

This can be one of the greatest examples of not knowing what to say and letting your mouth run on without paying attention. Whenever you are talking to a close friend or family member at the wake, funeral, or memorial service, do not say the following:

What NOT to Say or Do

- You look tired. Are you sleeping okay?
- It should have been me. I don't know why God didn't take me instead.
- Do you know what you're going to do with the house?

- How much of this is the life insurance policy taking care of?
- Who gets the car?
- Did you get the final copy of the will? I hope I get my fair share.
- Why are they here? I can't stand them.
- They are in a better place.
- God needed another lily for His flower garden. (No He didn't and no He doesn't.)
- How do you feel about burying your child?
- Another one bites the dust.
- I'm just here to meet people.
- He owes me money.
- I can't believe you are burying them in that outfit.
- What are we doing after this?
- Her side of the family shouldn't have come; they have been divorced for years.
- I never really liked them anyway.
- At least they're not in pain anymore.
- Do not give the family members a plant like ivy or plant that is expected to live a long time. It is best to give flowers like roses, lilies, tulips, etc. You do not want to give them a gift that will continually remind them of their loss.
- Your loss is heaven's gain.

Of course some of these were listed to help lighten the mood around funerals. They are still valid things to not say at or around a funeral. Plus, you'd be surprised what some people say when they don't know what to say.

Start of Service

We are gathered here today to honor the life and the memory of _____ (fill in the deceased name).

_____ was born in (fill in city and state) on _____ (fill in date) on a (describe day and time) _____. He was the oldest, youngest, etc. He grew up in _____ and always knew he would want to be a _____.

After high school, he went on to _____ (name of university). While he was there he met _____ (spouse's name). They were later married and had _____ children.

To some he was known as a _____ (fill in positive adjective) and to others he was always _____ (fill in positive adjective).

He was a great father, friend, and boss. (Adjust to be applicable to the deceased.)

In your time with the family, you will find out what information they would like you to share. Please keep in mind and make specific notes on what they would like you to say. In their time of loss and grieving, the last thing you want to do is make them upset at the funeral or graveside.

Words from Family and Friends

Having talked to the family in preparation for this service, they have asked different family members to share memories and a more personal side of the deceased. (Have an outline of who is speaking, reminding them beforehand to share funny and lighter stories of their loved one. Stories that will lighten the environment in the room, cause a small laugh, or a moment to relax are nice.)

Scriptures as Text for Service

"Jesus said to his disciples: 'Do not let your hearts be troubled. Believe in God, believe also in me. In my Father's house there are many dwelling places. If it were not so, would I have told you that I go to prepare a place for you? And if I go and prepare a place for you, I will come again and will take you to myself, so that where I am, there you may be also. And you know the way to the place where I am going.' Thomas said to him, 'Lord, we do not know where you are going. How can we know the way?' Jesus said to him, 'I am the way, and the truth, and the life. No one comes to the Father except through me.'" John 14:1-6

"No, in all these things we are more than conquerors through him who loved us. For I am convinced that neither death, nor life, nor angels, nor rulers, nor things present, nor things to come, nor powers, nor height, nor depth, nor anything else in all creation, will be able to separate us from the love of God in Christ Jesus our Lord." Romans 8:31

"I eagerly expect and hope that I will in no way be
ashamed, but will have sufficient courage so that
now as always Christ will be exalted in my body,
whether by life or by death. For to me, to live is
Christ and to die is gain. If I am to go on living
in the body, this will mean fruitful labor for me.
Yet what shall I choose? I do not know! I am torn
between the two; I desire to depart and be with
Christ, which is better by far." Philippians 1:20–23

In Philippians, we find such great encouragement. We know that this life is not meant to last forever. We know that life truly is just a vapor. We know that the greatest part of our destiny is to join Jesus in heaven with our Father God. I know that the loss of _____ (fill in name) is not something that anyone here would have wanted.

He will be greatly missed, but he would not want his death to be in vain. He would want me to share with you his undeniable faith and urgency to share his Christian faith with everyone he came in contact with.

I want to give you the opportunity that he would want you to have in this moment of life. It is no secret that _____ (fill in name) was a strong believer and he would want to make sure that you do not miss out on eternity with our Father God.

If you would like to receive Jesus into your heart and to know Him the same way _____ (fill in the name) did, repeat after me.

Find the natural break in the prayer and allow time for people to repeat after you. Do not speak quickly or use too many words in the phrase. Speaking slowly allows those repeating after you time to think about the words and the commitment they are making.

Prayer for Salvation

Father, I have sinned. I ask You to separate this sin from me and never hold it against me again. I ask You to come into my life, to be my Lord and Savior. Lead me and guide my by Your Holy Spirit. In Jesus name, amen.

If anyone has said that prayer for the first time, or would like more information on what it means to be a Christian, please let me know and we can set up a time to talk in the next few days.

I thank you all for coming and honoring the memory and life of _____ (fill in name).

Dismissal

- The family has arranged a small graveside service and would like to invite you to attend. Thank you for honoring their wishes and continuing to cover them in your prayers.

- The family has arranged a small graveside service and they have asked for it to be immediate family members only. Thank you for honoring their wishes and continuing to cover them in your prayers.

Notes

Healing

- Mental illness caused by trauma
- To heal
- curse any & all trauma - go
- remove diagnosed label
- command damage to go
- ungo
- command chemicals in body to be restored
- curse migraine (illness)
- health & wholeness into head, entire system - whole - needs afford to flow no more migraine
- listen to spirit
- let person be child - restitution of what was taken

- if Jesus praying for someone - person in audience has some pray for it - take it - don't limit God

- command arch or foot to be restored

multiple forms of abuse - mental, physical, sexual, ...

Method: info about our back right ailments

Notes

- command

- Carpel tunnel - jerky & thumb together - pull - no strength - restore
- chemicals to return to proper harmony & balance
- whole new set of intestines
- new vertebra, height, all the way down the spine
- curse every "free. or"? prion (?)
- command all vertebra to line up
-   "   sleepless nights to go
- restore the memory, strength & wholeness to mind
- speak restoration in ...
- strength in .. (you will be able to rest)

Knee replacement
- hands on knees for &
- curse any & all trauma
- effect of stress be gone
- everything normal function or
- blood pressure return to normal
- height to be restored
command - all pain to go
- curse headaches, never again
- ... to go
- health & wholeness in ...

Notes

Cancer

- curse it
- command it to go
- call for restoration
- curse "prion", has no nucleus -
  only cell with none -
- prions are bad cells that
  eat good cell
- doctors say prions are demonic

- curse all four spirit of cancer,
  throughout body
- speak brand new ...
- curse damage ...
- assignment of death taken off

Headache
- put hand on head
- other hand on heart
- curse trauma " trauma to head
- curse pain
- command it to go & not come back

Notes

Burning in stomach/intestines:

- from stress mostly, get rid of it, not spouse
- hand on chest & abdomen area
- health & wholeness into...
- cure IBS, Chron's disease, ph balance restored
- all pain to go
- problems swallowing to go

Shoulder Rotator Cuff:
- command fair scar tissue to go

Ear pain:
- hand in area
- new tonsils, lymph nodes to go down
- vertigo to go, infections go
- hearing loss be restored

Thank you John - up & down,
                   back & forth

Notes

Diabetes

- hand on pancreas
- ask it command to go
- new pancreas in Jesus name

www.joanhunter.org